Jimmy Carter's Betrayal of the South

Jeffrey St. John

Green Hill Publishers, Inc.
Ottawa, IL 61350

JIMMY CARTER'S BETRAYAL OF THE SOUTH

Green Hill Publishers, Inc.
Post Office Box 738
Ottawa, Illinois 61350

Library of Congress Catalogue Card Number: 76-40566
Manufactured in the United States of America
ISBN: 0-916054-40-3

CONTENTS

"Governments are like revolutions; you may put them into motion, but I defy you to control them *after* they are in motion."

—John Randolph of Roanoke (1773-1833)

Introduction

Will the South commit political, social and economic suicide by helping elect Jimmy Carter President?

"We went with Carter," said Selina Burch of the Communications Workers of America, District 3 of Atlanta, Georgia, "to beat Wallace and change the economic outlook for the South, to bring a new image."[1]

The current "image" of the South, Southwest, and West—sometimes referred to as the Sunbelt—without widespread and strong unions, is highly attractive to growing numbers of industries and individuals. In fact, the past two decades has witnessed a shift in population that has broad ramifications for the future.

"As the United States prepares to enter its third century," observed *The New York Times,* "a restless and historic movement is taking place, shifting people away from the Northern states that have been the base of population and power since the nation's infancy. The Census Bureau estimates of population changes in metropolitan areas between 1970 and 1974 show a continuation of patterns of enormous growth in the 'boom' areas of the South and Southwest and a slowing of growth, an end to growth, or even a loss of population in older Northern cities."[2]

The major cause for this radical shift of industry and population has been liberal governments' policies of taxing and regulating the productive private sector for the benefit of the nonproductive public sector. These destructive policies have been the foundation of northern liberalism for over four decades. Their consequences have been to drive the most productive factors out of the major urban areas, either to the suburbs or south to the states of the Sunbelt, where governments put a premium on the private sector and adopt a conservative approach to political rule. At the same time, the financial, social and political crises of cities like New York are clear evidence that modern liberalism is in a state of decay and collapse.

Jimmy Carter, the Southerner, was nominated for the presidency in New York by a political party that has been and continues to be dominated by a liberal philosophy. In order to secure the nomination it was necessary for Carter to agree to many of the proposals favored by Northern liberals and their allies in the American trade-union movement. One such proposal was the repeal of Right-to-Work Laws, now sanctioned by Section 14B of the Taft-Hartley Law. Such laws guarantee the right of a worker to join or not join a union. The right-to-work laws in force in virtually every southern state have prevented a takeover of industry and politics there by union bosses. In fact, the South has become a refuge for industries driven out of the North by political and economic chaos caused largely by unrestrained union monopoly power!

Bound up in Carter's drive for the presidency is a historic North-South confrontation for control of the political future. The political coalition of liberals, unions and other groups that gave Carter the nomination cannot elect him; only a combination of a liberal North and a nominally conservative solid South can. Yet the very policies he is pledged to pursue appear destructive to the long-range interests of the South, indeed of all the Sunbelt states. Put another way, a Carter victory would impose upon the South the very liberal policies that have driven industries and population from the Northeast to the more conservative Sunbelt.

Carter's quest for the presidency thus solves a crucial problem of Northern liberals, for their goal of continued control of the country has been eroded by the shift of industry and population to the South. A Carter victory in 1976 would usher in an administration led by various liberal-to-left activist groups who have long pleaded for vast government powers over the private sector of industry and over middle-class Americans. In short, Carter appears to be leading a coalition of political and economic radicals who would go far beyond the massive expansion of the powers of the federal government Franklin Roosevelt instituted in 1933.

As a southern son, Carter in his bid for the political power of the presidency is making a radical break with a long political tradition. This southern tradition extends back to the southern founders of America—to Thomas Jefferson, James Madison, and others who came to have a pessimism toward political power and a healthy distrust for those who sought to use it. The Virginia planter-statesman, John Randolph of Roanoke, relatively unknown outside the South, summed up this southern tradition of fierce opposition to centralized government when he observed that governments are like revolutions: once they are set into motion they are impossible to control.

The current, out-of-control federal and bureaucratic government would appear to be a vindication of that viewpoint, first expressed in 1829.

Much has been made of the fact that Jimmy Carter is the first southerner since Zachary Taylor in the 1850s to be nominated by a national party for the presidency, and that this somehow represents the emergence of a "New South." The historical fact remains, however, that no southern leader since Taylor has been nominated because most of the leaders distrusted the federal government and believed passionately in the concept of States' Rights.

The late U.S. Senator Richard Russell (Democrat, Georgia), is a case in point. No one in Washington who remembers Russell, including Carter who has praised him, would deny that he had all the qualities and qualifications to be president. However, Russell firmly believed in the Founding Fathers' concept of limited government and noninterference of the federal government in the affairs of the states. At the same time, his own party was dominated by northern political liberal leaders who believed in the vigorous use of federal power. Russell was thereby denied a chance to be president, not because he was a southerner, but because he was a constitutional conservative.

As governor of Georgia in the 1930s, before he became a U.S. Senator, Russell put his conservative philosophy into practice when he reorganized the state government, slashing the number of state agencies from 107 to 18, saving taxpayers millions of dollars.[3] Not until Carter became chief executive of that state was a similar reorganization attempted, and as we shall see, Carter failed in the effort because his political philosophy was liberal, not conservative. At the same time he won his four-year term as Georgia governor in 1970 by running as a conservative—only to switch once elected. This was clearly the technique he employed during the presidential primaries, projecting a conservative anti-Washington-big-government image, only to embrace a party and a platform calling for more, not less, government. "You can sum up this party platform in two words: more government," observed Bill Moyers, former aide to President Lyndon B. Johnson.[4]

Jimmy Carter's compulsion to gain the vast powers of the presidency and his plan to use that power are coming at a time when the nation has been profoundly shaken and disillusioned by the abuse of power by past presidents. Carter proposes to restore faith and trust in government—government that southern founders like Thomas Jefferson came to believe could only govern best if it governed least. Ironically, Carter's power drive comes in the year of the Bicentennial of Jefferson's Declaration of Independence from a powerful, bureaucratic, centralized British government that had grown abusive and tyrannical. "History and political experience," observed historian Carl Becker, "convinced Jefferson that man had been governed too much by kings claiming Divine Right."[5]

Former U.S. Senator Eugene McCarthy, a liberal Democrat from Minnesota, told this writer in an interview shortly before Carter was nominated that he feared the former Georgia governor "supported the somewhat aggressive and imperial presidency" and that his talk of marrying theology with presidential power in the name of reestablishing the national moral leadership was a throwback to the concept of the Divine Right of Kings doctrine. "I think it's good," said the independent candidate for president in 1976, "for a president to assert some moral leadership, but when he begins to talk about himself as being the one voice that can speak for the country, I think you've got to worry about him.

"I don't mind his trying to provide moral leadership, but this is like Henry VIII, sort of: I'm the head of the church and the state both and I am the moral leader of the country, and I'm the voice. I don't think he should say he speaks for the country."[6]

Jimmy Carter is the first presidential candidate in modern times openly to advocate the marriage of his private religious convictions with the vast public powers of the presidency. In the past, the religious convictions of the President have always remained a private matter. Also, one of the great strengths of Christianity has been the doctrine of personal salvation for those who turned, not to the leadership of government for their moral values and guidance, but to a religious credo *separate* from the secular state. Carter clearly is espousing a doctrine of moral salvation through politics. Without realizing it, perhaps, this is also a form of idolatry.

Jimmy Carter's claim on the power of the presidency is based exclusively on a high moral standard that he has set for himself and commands us to follow. But as the evidence will show, that standard is shot through with contradictions; the power he would employ would be open to reckless abuse because the words and actions of the candidate himself and his closest advisors do not match their moral claims.

NOTES

1. "Georgian Labor Leaders Intensely Loyal to Carter," *Times-Advertiser* (Trenton, N.J.) May 27, 1976.
2. "Sunbelt Region Leads Nation in Growth of the Population," *The New York Times*, Feb. 8, 1976.
3. Leslie Wheeler, *Jimmy Who?* (Woodbury, N.Y.: Barron's, 1976).
4. Democratic National Convention, New York City. Reported on CBS-TV, July 13, 1976, 9:38 pm EDT.
5. Carl Becker, "What is still living in the political philosophy of Thomas Jefferson?" in Merrill D. Peterson, Ed., *Thomas Jefferson, A Profile* (New York: Hill and Wang, 1967).
6. Eugene McCarthy, interview with Maury Povich and Jeffrey St. John, Washington, D.C. (WTTG-TV) July 11, 1976.

"This vote in Florida was the
first test of strength in the South."
—Jimmy Carter
(November 17, 1975)

1

The Watergating of George Wallace

It was the afternoon of December 8, 1975. My wife was saying that Jimmy Carter's press secretary, Joseph (Jody) Powell, was on the phone from Atlanta, "threatening to sue, if you don't issue a retraction."

I took the phone. Powell was angry and ugly, in a sweet, southern way. He demanded a public retraction to a broadcast commentary heard throughout North Carolina on November 28. It charged that the Carter campaign rigged a straw poll at a November 16 Florida State Democratic Convention in Orlando. It also charged that for two years four principal aides of former Georgia Governor Carter had their expenses paid by the Democratic National Committee. "Clearly evidence," we said in the commentary, "that the Democrats have been grooming Governor Carter for two years as the man to stop Wallace."[1]

The three national TV networks, the two national wire services, and a number of influential newspapers played the results of the Florida straw poll as a major news story. The media contended that Carter's win over Wallace, who came in third, was a forecast of trouble for the Alabama governor. The news stories also projected Carter as a rising national political star. The Florida straw poll was critical since it gave Carter's bandwagon its initial and most important political push toward the 1976 nomination in New York City in July.

Remarkably, Powell did not dispute the charges of the poll rigging and a stacked convention of pro-Carter delegates. "You know, Mr. St. John," he said on the telephone, "that's politics." What alarmed Powell was the charge that Carter aides were using Democratic National Committee money—a fact that would not sit well with a field of other Democratic presidential hopefuls in the 1976 primaries. DNC Chairman Robert Strauss could be charged with using his office to favor one candidate over others.

Powell demanded the names (Hamilton Jordan, Knox Pitts, Rick Hutcheson and Marc Cutright). He was noticeably disturbed when I informed him that I had written a longer story on the entire affair for my newspaper syndicate.[2] The tone of the conversation changed considerably, as he apparently realized he could not resort to a government agency to intimidate me. To influence a broadcast journalist he could have invoked the Federal Communications Commission, the controlling agency, which requires a broadcaster to offer right of reply when the integrity of an individual or organization is questioned on the "public airwaves." Not so with a newspaper columnist.

Powell denied the allegation that the Democratic National Committee was paying Carter's four aides. "As I stated to you on the phone," I wrote to him on that day, following up our conversation, "I would be willing to issue a retraction in my column and in my regular 'Viewpoint' commentary on WRAL-TV, Raleigh, North Carolina, if I am provided a notarized statement that they have not had their expenses or salaries paid by the Democratic National Committee in the last 24 months, and a notarized statement from Governor Carter's finance chairman that no one else in the Governor's campaign committee has received payment of any kind from the DNC."[3]

Jody Powell never responded to my request. Nor did he accept the opportunity by WRAL-TV President James Goodmon to reply to my charges![4]

The encounter provides an insight into the character of

Powell and, in turn, Jimmy Carter. The press secretary is regarded as "one of Carter's closest advisers . . . and plays a key role in speechwriting and strategy planning for the campaign."[5] It also raises grave questions about Carter's presidential campaign of integrity, through which he has risen from the unknown who first ran for Governor of Georgia in 1966 to the Democratic nominee for president in 1976.

This author is not the only journalist to raise doubts about Jimmy Carter's claim to honesty and the integrity of his closest campaign aides. For example, during the same month of that personal encounter with Jody Powell, Steven Brill, contributing editor of *New York* magazine, was traveling extensively with Carter. In March 1976 he published his observations in the liberal monthly, *Harper's*. The article, "Jimmy Carter's Pathetic Lies," was a shocking indictment of the former Georgia governor, members of his staff, and some of the means used to achieve the end, the nomination. "His is the most sincerely insincere, politically antipolitical, and slickly unslick campaign of the year," Brill wrote. "Using an image that is a hybrid of honest, simple Abe Lincoln and charming, idealistic John Kennedy, he has packaged himself to take the idol-seekers for a long ride."

Brill's most shocking charge was that while Carter was governor of Georgia, his organization tampered with his public record; "Governor Carter and his people censored documents, especially speeches, that should be in the public record,"[6] he quotes an archives librarian.

Powell managed to have an advance look at Brill's article and successfully orchestrated a countercampaign that, according to *Harper's* editor Lewis Lapham, "masterminded a backlash against the piece before it was ever published."[7] The Archives Director in Atlanta issued a formal statement denying Brill's quotations from his staff about missing public speeches, but Brill said he would stand behind his story.[8]

My own experience with the Carter people in November 1975 corresponds with those of other journalists and columnists from *The Boston Globe, The New York Times, National Observer,* and *Harper's.* Editor Lapham summed up our suspicions about the aloof loner Carter when he stated, "The managers of the campaign to discredit Brill went about their work with an eagerness reminiscent of the tactics used by the Nixon Administration."[9]

The tactics a person is prepared to employ can often provide a clue to his true character, even when carefully concealed beneath a façade of religious faith and promises never to tell a lie.

NOTES

1. Jeffrey St. John, "Viewpoint" No. 3229, November 28, 1975, WRAL-TV, WRAL-FM and the North Carolina News Network. (Complete text reproduced in Appendix 1.)
2. "Watergating of George Wallace," Copley News Service, November 28, 1975. (Complete text reproduced in Appendix 2.)
3. Letter to Jody Powell, December 8, 1975. (Complete text reproduced in Appendix 3.)
4. Letter from James Goodmon, President, WRAL-TV, Capitol Broadcasting Company, Raleigh, N.C., November 28, 1975.
5. "The Powell Behind Carter," *Newsweek,* June 21, 1976.
6. "Jimmy Carter's Pathetic Lies—The Heroic Image Is Made of Brass," *Harper's,* March 1976.
7. "The Powell Behind Carter," *Newsweek.*
8. "Deny Carter Dirty Tricks," *Atlanta Constitution,* Feb. 5, 1976.
9. Quoted in *National Journal,* May 29, 1976, from *Harper's,* May 1976.

"I know Jimmy writes how poor we were, but really we were never poor."
—"Miss Lillian" Carter, interview (May 21, 1976)

2

The Ambition of a Barefoot Boy

The southern, small-town, barefoot-poor boyhood portrait that Jimmy Carter conveys in his autobiography, *Why Not the Best?* has a personal and political appeal among millions of Americans, southerners and northerners alike, because it is basically American and so southern. It fixes in our mind the place where Carter began and by contrast shows how far he has come since his poor-boy childhood in the southern Georgia. "For years we used an outdoor privy in the back yard for sanitation," he writes, "and a hand pump for water supply."[1]

During the primaries, he referred repeatedly to his poor boyhood. "I come from one of the poorest parts of the country," he said during the Florida contest. "In my county we don't have a doctor, we don't have a pharmacist, a dentist. . . ."[2] In an interview shortly after his victory in Ohio and defeat in California on June 8, he told a reporter about his special relationship with the poor of America. "I do have a unique experience," he said. "One of the strongest and best of these is my relationship with poor people. That's where I came from. That's where I lived. These are my people. Not only whites but particularly blacks. It's not an accident that (Congressman) Andy Young and Daddy King [Martin Luther King, Sr.] support me. They know that I understand their problems. They know that I've demonstrated an eagerness to solve them."[3]

Carter's mother, however, conveys a different impression of his poor, barefoot boyhood. "I know Jimmy writes about how poor we were," Miss Lillian Carter said during the primaries, "but really we were never poor. There was no running water or electricity but no one in the country had lights unless they built it on their own. We were just like all country people. *We didn't feel poor* and we always had a car. We had the first radio in Plains. We had the first TV set."[4] (Author's emphasis.)

Most southerners, white and black, know precisely what is meant by the phrase *"We never felt poor."* So do those first and second-generation Americans of immigrant parents who came to this country around the turn of the century, bringing with them a spiritual-cultural tradition for which physical comforts and conveniences were never a substitute. "We didn't have much money," stated Miss Lillian, "but we had everything we needed. Jimmy's book [*Why Not the Best?*] makes us sound so poor you want to get out a hat and take up a collection."[5]

Jimmy Carter's attitude toward being poor and what should be done to solve "being poor" seems more northern liberal than southern conservative. In his autobiography, however, he writes of his own hard work as a farm boy, his enterprise in selling peanuts, and his remarkable skill, at nine years old, when he saved enough money to purchase five bales of cotton, which he then sold at a handsome profit. "I sold it for enough money," he writes, "to purchase five houses, owned at the time by the estate of the recently deceased local undertaker. From then until I left home to enter the Naval Academy, I collected $16.50 in rent each month from those five houses."[6]

His youthful attitude toward government was less independent in spirit: "We learned to appreciate the stability of the agriculture programs brought about by federal government action," he recalls, "and we cooperated fully in the soil and water conservation service plans for erosion control and the enhancement of wildlife. But my father never forgave President Franklin Roosevelt for requiring that hogs be slaughtered and cotton be plowed up when these production control programs first went into effect. He never again voted for Roosevelt."[7]

Carter records, moreover, that while it is difficult for him to decide when he first became interested in politics, he remembers during the Great Depression of the 1930s "political decisions in Washington had an immediate and direct effect on our lives. Farm programs, Rural Electrification, Works Progress Administration, Civilian Conservation Corps and others were of immense personal importance."[8]

He even recalls that "Daddy always encouraged me to attend the political rallies in surrounding neighborhoods and towns even when he could not go himself . . . the year before his death [he] was elected to the state legislature. My father served only one year, but it was a thrill for him."[9]

Although there may not have been any specific moment when Jimmy Carter became interested in a political career, the Carter family apparently has always maintained an intense interest in politics. Carter's grandfather was an avid supporter of Tom Watson, a firebrand, nationally-known populist from southern Georgia; Miss Lillian speaks to this day of Watson with reverence, affection and even love.

Jimmy Carter's political ambitions may have their roots in his barefoot boyhood in southern Georgia, but his perception of politics and how power should be used is northern—even though his style seems southern. This perception may be due to the often-overlooked fact that Carter was not educated in the South, but at the U.S. Naval Academy at Annapolis—hardly a traditional southern education.

His northern-like view to solving problems is at sharp contrast with that of Tom Watson. As the late historian, southern-born Richard M. Weaver, observed, Watson was distinguished by his hostility to northern financial and political power because of the South's vulnerability to exploitation by those from without as well as those from within. "He [Watson] saw, moreover, that there was a group among his own people," Weaver wrote, "willing to become the instruments of Northern domination while wearing the garb of sectional loyalty. To betray an ideal at the very moment one praises it is an ancient ruse, and some of those who talked most glibly of the antebellum South were the readiest to drive a bargain with Northern financial imperialism."[10]

Carter's ambition to be the elected head of a strong national government, which southerners have fought from the Republic's beginning, can only be achieved by powerful northern political alliances of the sort Watson abhorred.

And even with his promise to "cure" problems like poverty we find an unsouthern attitude. One of the great strengths of southerners, white or black, during the past century has been that they have been able to endure great adversity. The southerner, while he may have seemed poor in material goods, has always found refuge in a rich and diverse spiritual and cultural traditions and values. There is no indication that Carter understands this spirit in his writings or speeches, although clearly, as most southerners know, there is a difference between poverty of the body and poverty of the spirit and culture.

Richard Weaver drew the clear distinction between the southerner's looking inward to the spiritual man and the nonsoutherner's always looking outward to the external, material man. "The South has kept something," he observed, "of the attitude of the soldier: aware of the battle, he has only contempt for the tender, querulous, agitated creature of modern artifice, sighing for comforts he is 'entitled to' and protesting that the world cannot really be like this."[11]

NOTES

1. Jimmy Carter, *Why Not the Best?* (New York: Bantam Books, 1976) pp 7-8.
2. Robert W. Turner, Ed., *"I'll Never Lie to You": Jimmy*

Carter in His Own Words (New York: Ballantine Books, 1976), p. 14.
3. *"I'll Never Lie to You,"* p. 20.
4. "The Raising of Jimmy," *New York Post,* May 21, 1976.
5. "Her Son Jimmy Wore His Cap to Bed," *People,* July 19, 1976.
6. *Why Not the Best?* p. 22.
7. *Why Not the Best?* p. 17.
8. *Why Not the Best?* p. 85.
9. *Why Not the Best?* p. 86.
10. Richard M. Weaver, *The Southern Tradition at Bay* (New Rochelle, N.Y.: Arlington House, 1968), p. 386.
11. *The Southern Tradition at Bay.* p. 34.

"I became most disillusioned with
the Navy, and the military in general."
—Jimmy Carter,
Why Not the Best?

3

A Life Beyond the Land

Since the founding of Jamestown, Virginia, in 1607, land has always had a special, almost mystical meaning for Americans. In the South, land owned or share cropped has a significance that finds its roots in Sunday Bible School lessons that teach reverence for the values of God, family and work on the land.

Jimmy Carter's political campaign biography is the most poetic and the most genuine when he writes of his boyhood love of the land in southern Georgia. Despite this genuine affection, however, he broke with the land and the South as a young teenager, when he set his life course for a career with the Navy after his father, through a local Congressman, secured his appointment to the U.S. Naval Academy at Annapolis. Why?

He may have offered an answer when he wrote, "During my childhood I never considered myself a part of the Plains society, but always thought of myself as a visitor when I entered that 'metropolitan' community."[1]

At Annapolis, Carter came to appreciate classical music at a period in the 1940s when the nation at war was "swinging" to the Big Bands and the South was stomping its feet to country-western music, sometimes crudely described in those days as hillbilly music. "My roommate and I," he writes, "spent most of our meager money on classical phonograph records. Other midshipmen would visit our room and we would argue for hours about the relative quality of performance of orchestras and concert soloists."[2]

A remarkable degree of sophistication for a southern farm boy! Perhaps Carter wanted to demonstrate that the South was cultured and worldly. Southerners have always lived with the northern stereotype of the South as ignorant and uncultured, while secretly harboring the conviction that the northerners were the real infidels and cultural barbarians.

Even today, this break with his southern cultural background manifests itself. For example, as a Southern Baptist, "born-again" Christian, Carter most often quotes Reinhold Niebuhr, a New England-born liberal theologian who, after his break with socialism, taught for 32 years at the Union Theological Seminary in New York.[3] Another nonsoutherner and non-American Carter calls on frequently for theological inspiration is the East German-born theologian Paul Tillich, who was a Socialist in Germany from 1919 to 1933. Opposing German National Socialism (Nazism), Tillich fled to America and also taught at Union Theological Seminary. He later moved on to the faculty at Harvard and was at the University of Chicago at the time of his death in 1965. A lesser theological reference for Carter is the Swiss-born, but liberal, theologian Karl Barth, who stayed in Europe and taught in Germany. Barth was particularly vigorous in his denunciation of a "narrow anti-Communist crusade."[4] Needless to say, these liberal, European religious philosophers are viewed with a great deal of suspicion by the fundamentalist Baptist brotherhood Carter claims as his own.

Carter's choice of cultural heros in poetry and music is perhaps even stranger and more unsouthern than in philosophy. He loves, for example, the poetry of the Welsh-born Dylan Thomas, who, although a great poet, lived a life of despair and died in New York of an overdose of hard liquor in 1953.[5] In philosophy, Carter refers most frequently to the Danish-born, nineteenth-century thinker, Søren Kierkegaard, who died five years before the U.S. Civil War. In music, his tastes run to such favorites of the New Left 1960s counterculture as Bob Dylan, who was born in Minnesota and with whom Carter has a personal relationship. "I really like rock music," Carter insists, despite the fact he comes from a region where Johnny Cash is country and western king, "and Bob Dylan and I get along really well."[6]

His relationship with hard rock singer Gregg Allman is stranger still. For example, in a Macon, Georgia, courtroom on June 23 and 24, 1976, Allman testified, under immunity from prosecution, that he received hard drugs including cocaine. "I used about one-half gram a day," Allman told the court.[7] "I care for these people," Carter states of Allman and Dylan, "and I respect them. . . . They are strange kids and yet they look on me with love. There is a closeness I feel to these young people."[8]

Carter's friendship with rock music groups has been so personal and close that through May 15 it netted his presidential campaign $139,780.41—of which $64,031.50 came from an Allman Brothers Band Concert.[9]

These contradictions—his movement from classical music in the 1940s to counterculture folk music and hard rock in the 1970s, and his devotion to the liberal theological views of Niebuhr and Tillich while courting the southern fundamentalist Baptists—have one consistency: they are nonsouthern in origin.

Another baffling mystery is Carter's naval career. With his characteristic intensity he studied and worked hard to gain admission to Annapolis and he graduated 59th in his class of 820.[10] But once in the regular post-World War II Navy things turned sour. "I became most disillusioned with the Navy, and the military in general, and would have probably resigned had not I and all Annapolis graduates been serving 'at the pleasure of the President.' "[11] At the same time, however, when he transferred to submarines he found it a great adventure and was apparently a competent officer. And when he met the future Admiral Hyman Rickover, sometimes called the Father of the Nuclear Navy, and transfered to the then-infant nuclear-powered Navy: "My job was the best and most promising in the Navy and the work was challenging and worthwhile. The salary was good, and the retirement benefits were liberal and assured. The contact with Admiral Rickover alone made it worthwhile."[12]

But, he soon reveals, "after some tortuous days" he resigned in 1953 to go back to Plains, Georgia, with the death of his father as the reason. Yet the decision provoked his wife Rosalynn to violent disagreement. Carter says, "She did not, she protested, wish to go back to the restrictive life of our home in Plains, where our families lived and where our married freedom might be cramped or partially dominated by relatives, particularly her mother and my mother."[13]

Stranger still is the tribute paid to Rickover. "He may have never cared or known it, certainly not at that time, but Admiral Rickover had a profound effect on my life—perhaps more than anyone except my own parents."[14]

Nevertheless, despite this "profound" influence, which might make an average person remain to work closely with a person who had so influenced him, Carter resigned.

Jimmy Carter had had his unsouthern character set by the Navy and by Rickover. What is it in that character that drove him to leave the wider world, with a potential goal of Chief of Naval Operations, for the small, confining world of Plains, Georgia?

NOTES

1. *Why Not the Best?* p. 15.
2. *Why Not the Best?* pp. 45-46.
3. *Encyclopedia Britannica,* (Chicago: University of Chicago, 1974), 15th Ed., Vol. VII, p. 334.
4. *Micropaedia* (Chicago: University of Chicago, 1974), Vol. I, p. 842.
5. *Micropaedia,* Vol. IX, p. 960.
6. Jimmy Carter, interview with Sally Quinn, "Behind the Grin of the Peanut Farmer from Georgia," *Washington Post,* March 28, 1976.
7. "Allman Testifies in Drug Probe, Admits Cocaine Use," *Rolling Stone,* July 19, 1976.

8. "Behind the Grin," *Washington Post.*
9. Federal Election Commission records, Campaign statements dated 3/19/75, 10/3/75, 11/25/75, 2/21/76, 1/14/76, 5/3/76, 5/19/76, 5/19/76, 5/17/76, Washington, D.C.
10. *Why Not the Best?* p. 64.
11. *Why Not the Best?* p. 50.
12. *Why Not the Best?* pp. 64-65.
13. *Why Not the Best?* p. 70.
14. *Why Not the Best?* p. 61.

"We feared and respected him
and strove to please him."
—Jimmy Carter
on Admiral Hyman Rickover,
Why Not the Best?

4

A Case Study in Character

Jimmy Carter is really two people: the public, smiling, soft-spoken candidate, speaking of love and compassion, is one. The other, according to friendly biographers Howard Norton and Bob Slosser, is "a tough, impatient executive who demands, and gets, both hard work and excellence from those who work for him. . . .

"This is not to say that Carter's friendliness is a political 'put on' or that the smile is artificial . . ." the authors continue. "The point is that there are two Jimmy Carters—both of them the real thing. And when you vote for one, you get both."[1]

Former McGovern speechwriter and briefly a speechwriter for Carter, Robert Shrum provides a much harsher view. "I never saw him smile in private," he observed after he quit, charging that the candidate was a hypocrite, "unless there was someone there he wanted to impress. Carter is a man of iron control."[2]

The private Jimmy Carter bears a striking resemblance to the man he credits with having as much influence on his life as his parents, Admiral Hyman C. Rickover. "We feared and respected him," Carter writes of Rickover, "and strove to please him. I do not in that period remember his every saying a complimentary word to me. The absence of a comment was his compliment. . . ."[3]

While governor, and as a presidential candidate, Carter

in private seems to copy Rickover's aloof, cold and ruthlessly efficient character. Rickover forced the men who worked under him to strive and aim their sights high. Carter aimed to be Chief of Naval Operations but, strangely, exchanged that goal for a narrower world in Plains, Georgia. "Did I want to be the Chief of Naval Operations," he recalled later in an interview, "and devote my whole life to that one narrowly defined career, which was a good one—or did I want to go back and build a more diverse life with a lot of friends, permanent stability in a community, and interrelationship in the life of a whole group of people. . . ."[4]

A naval officer who did become Chief of Naval Operations in 1970 was Admiral Elmo R. Zumwalt, Jr. Now retired and active in Virginia Democratic politics, Zumwalt presented the party platform plank on national defense at the 1976 convention that nominated Carter. Zumwalt's extensive dealings with Rickover, or "Rick" as he is known, may provide a clue to Carter's own true character and how he would act as President. "Rick is not subtle," observed Zumwalt, "just devious."[5]

Zumwalt contends that Rickover is the most powerful Navy politician in Washington, with the power to defy even the Secretary of the Navy. He cites, for example, Rickover's ability to get his political friends in Congress to extend his tenure as head of the Navy's Division of Nuclear Propulsion beyond the mandatory retirement age of 62. Rickover is now in his seventies. This is an unaccustomed break with the historical tradition, in which the U.S. military is subordinate to civilian authority. Zumwalt also claims Rickover sabotaged "my plans for modernizing the Navy" and asserts that he runs his department like a "totalitarian mini-state," often violating Navy regulations while severely punishing subordinates who violate his rules.

Zumwalt also contends that "Rick" once blackmailed a subordinate working on a new fleet plan by threatening to scuttle his sought-after command of the carrier U.S.S. *Enterprise* if a recommendation for nuclear ships was not included. In another instance, according to Zumwalt, Rickover actually ruined the Naval career of the commanding officer of the U.S. Naval Shipyard at Pearl Harbor, Hawaii, because the officer, Captain Charles O. Swanson, opposed a Rickover management plan. Zumwalt contends this behavior was "un-American and autocratic. . . . It was, to be blunt about it," Zumwalt writes, "a system of spying and intimidation. Members of Rickover's AEC [Atomic Energy Commission] shipyard inspection team walked around the yard, clipboards in hand, making notes on who was smoking and drinking a soda or talking to friends."[6]

When Carter was governor of Georgia, he gained the reputation for similar ruthlessness and a willingness to let his ends justify his means. "He never asked for any advice, any suggestions," observed Carter critic Tom Murphy, Speaker of the Georgia House, "he just gave orders."[7] A more balanced view is provided by biographer Leslie Wheeler in *Jimmy Who?* "During his term," she writes, "Carter also showed himself to be a highly impatient man. He wanted quick action, and when he didn't get it, he often took matters in his own hands."[8]

Like Rickover, Carter has gotten the reputation for being vindictive and willing to pursue his critics with the power of government as an instrument of punishment. Former Georgia Governor Lester Maddox, whom Carter praised in the past, provided a personal experience that Carter does not like to be crossed. "He's cold, cunning, cruel," Maddox insists, "and will destroy anything or anyone who stands in his way. In my particular instance [as lieutenant governor], he told me in January 1971 that if I crossed him on any issue he would work to destroy me with the full resources at his command, and he spent four years working on it."[9]

Maddox, a one-time segregationist, has support for his view of Carter in the former editor of the *Atlanta Constitution*, Reg Murphy, who, as political editor for the paper, first met Carter in 1963.

". . . he is a mean, hard-eyed sort of fellow," remarked

Murphy, now editor of the San Francisco *Examiner*, "who tolerates nobody who opposes him. The governor just absolutely does not take challenges from anybody. I always figured that a man who would lower himself to get into a shouting match with Lester Maddox has a very low boiling point."[10]

Aides of Jimmy Carter privately contend that as President he would operate much like Admiral Rickover; they qualify this by saying that Carter would operate within the system. In fact, the former Georgia governor met with Rickover prior to announcing for the presidency "more to draw inspiration than to solicit advice."[11]

NOTES

1. Howard Norton and Bob Slosser, *The Miracle of Jimmy Carter* (Plainfield, N.J.: 1976), Logos International, p. 111.
2. "Giving Carter the Fish Eye," *Newsweek*, May 17, 1976.
3. *Why Not the Best?*, p. 61.
4. Interview, "Bill Moyers' Journal," Public Broadcasting System. Taped April 5, 1976, broadcast on PBS May 6, 1976.
5. Adm. Elmo R. Zumwalt, Jr., U.S.N. (Ret.) *On Watch—A Memoir* (New York: Quadrangle Books, The New York Times Book Co., 1976), p. 86.
6. Zumwalt, *On Watch—A Memoir*, p. 112.
7. "Who is Jimmy Carter?", Newspaper Enterprise Association, Feb. 10, 1976.
8. Leslie Wheeler *Jimmy Who?* (Woodbury, N.Y.: Barrons, 1976), p. 86.
9. "Jekyll and Hyde," *Newsweek*, July 19, 1976.
10. "Absolutely Ruthless," *Newsweek*, July 19, 1976.
11. "Rickover an Inspiration for Carter," *The News & Observer*, Raleigh, N.C., July 14, 1976, Jack Anderson with Les Whitten, column.

"I had run for governor and lost.
Everything I did was not gratifying."
—Jimmy Carter, interview
(May 6, 1976)

5

Plains as a Launching Platform

Annapolis for Jimmy Carter had apparently been a way out of Plains, Georgia, into a wider world that eventually did not fulfill his larger ambitions. When he resigned from the Navy in 1953 and returned to his small southern community, his perspective had been altered, but not his ambition.

"For Jimmy had been out of the state for over a decade," writes Leslie Wheeler of Carter when he became a state legislator, "and these years away had given him a different perspective. They had tended to reinforce the liberal and humanitarian values he had learned from his mother. Thus he was destined to be more than just another country politician, seeking to care for his own."[1]

Despite Carter's claims that the reason for his return to Plains was to take control of the family business and honor his father's memory with public service to the community, he had another reason. This was the specific purpose of launching a political career. He admits, for example, that on the death of his father, local county leaders urged his mother to fill his father's state senate seat. "When she refused," he writes, "one of my father's close friends was chosen to take the post, and he served for eight or ten years in the State House of Representatives. I would not have challenged him for the seat, although I thought about it several times during the ensuing years."[2]

In the nine years before he won a seat in the Georgia State Senate in 1962 (after his opponents sought to rig the returns and deny him the seat), Carter concentrated on his peanut business and kept his hand in politics by becoming chairman of the Sumter County School Board. This was the period shortly after the historic U.S. Supreme Court decision of 1954 that segregated schools were unconstitutional. "At no time during the six years he served on the board," writes Leslie Wheeler, "did he do anything to help enforce the Supreme Court decision outlawing segregation. . . . There is no doubt that, like the rest of the members of the board, Carter was a segregationist."[3] At the same time, he refused to join the White Citizens Council, a courageous decision in those days when the fever of massive resistance was at its height after the U.S. Supreme Court decision. But when he sought to offer the county school board a consolidation plan, which some charged was an integrationist ploy, he was defeated—the first defeat he suffered. This fight, however, gave Carter his first taste for political campaigning, which he has never lost.

"It was my first real venture into election politics, and campaigning," he remarked later, "and the failure of my effort was a stinging disappointment. My own community of Plains would have lost one of its schools, and my neighbors voted overwhelmingly against the school merger proposals. There was considerable bitterness in Plains because of my support of the consolidation plan."[4]

It is indicative of the political style he has followed most of his career that he fails to mention that this plan was perceived as one to effect integration. The rejection of the plan by his own neighbors was doubtless due to his refusal to join the White Citizens Council and his attempts to integrate his local church, as well as to the outspoken views of his mother on racial issues.

While Carter hates to lose, the defeats he has suffered have always acted as a spur to wider and higher ambitions. It was about this time that he decided to run for the

Georgia State Senate, when he began to perfect his theological approach to politics, which he later used in running for governor in 1966 and 1970. A local pastor sought to persuade him to enter the ministry rather than the dishonorable profession of politics. Carter countered, "How would you like to be the pastor of 80,000 members?" Carter then observed: "He finally admitted that it was possible to stay honest and at the same time minister to the needs of the 80,000 citizens of the 14th senate district."[5]

After successfully winning his State Senate seat, Carter began to build his reputation as a liberal of the "New South" and affected the style of then-popular President John F. Kennedy. "People noticed his trim and fit appearance," writes Leslie Wheeler, "and remarked on his resemblance to John F. Kennedy. There was the same shock of hair, the boyish grin, and the same seriousness and quiet humor. Carter even shared Kennedy's habit of emphasizing points with jabs of an open finger."[6]

His state senate race and, later, his 1966 gubernatorial effort were based on a campaign of running against the political bosses and the established power brokers. After an energetic Democratic primary campaign, Carter finished third behind Ellis Arnall and Lester Maddox. Maddox was selected governor by the state legislature after the general election had failed to secure a majority for any candidate. Carter's defeat was largely due to his liberal-progressive campaign and the fact that he was relatively unknown. Despite Carter's own negative and almost black depression toward the results, an analysis of the returns demonstrates that he did remarkably well for a political novice. But his reaction to his defeat is more significant than the defeat itself. "The entire experience was extremely disappointing to me," he later wrote. "I was deeply in debt, had lost twenty-two pounds (down to 130) and wound up with Lester Maddox as governor of Georgia."[7]

He said in 1976 that "I was going through a stage in my life that was a very difficult one. I had run for governor and lost. Nothing I did was gratifying. When I succeeded in something, I got no pleasure out of it. When I failed at something, it was a horrible experience for me."[8]

It was at this time that his sister, faith healer and evangelist Ruth Stapleton, contends that Carter underwent a religious conversion that made him a "born-again" Christian. "Ruth asked him if he would give up his life," writes Leslie Wheeler, "and everything that he owned for Christ, and he said he would. But when she asked him if he would be able to give up politics, he had to think for a long time before finally answering that he would not. His sister told him that he would never find peace until he was able to do this. She remembered him as being very emotional and crying, but he had no such memory."[9]

Carter waited only a month after his 1966 defeat and then plunged into a grueling four-year campaign for the governorship of Georgia. "I remembered the admonition," he states, " 'you show me a good loser and I will show you a loser.' I did not intend to lose again.

"From 1966 through 1970, I worked with more concentration and commitment than ever before in my life. I tried to expand my interests in as many different directions as possible, to develop my own seed business into a profitable and stable enterprise, and to evolve a carefully considered political strategy to win the governor's race in 1970."[10]

And it was a strategy that was radically different from the one he employed in his 1966 race.

NOTES

1. Leslie Wheeler, *Jimmy Who?* p. 35.
2. *Why Not the Best?* p. 87.
3. *Jimmy Who?* p. 39.
4. *Why Not the Best?* p. 88.
5. *Why Not the Best?* p. 89.
6. *Jimmy Who?* p. 39.

7. *Why Not the Best?* p. 112.
8. "Bill Moyers' Journal," May 6, 1976.
9. *Jimmy Who?* p. 138.
10. *Why Not the Best?* p. 112.

"Carter tailored his campaign to exploit . . . weaknesses."

—Numan V. Bartley and Hugh D. Graham, *Southern Politics and the Second Reconstruction*

6

The Outsider Becomes the Insider

Jimmy Carter's secret for political success, from the time he first ran for public office, has been due less to his own strengths than to the weaknesses of his opponents. His formula is simply to attack "the establishment" and the "political bosses and insiders" as a powerless outsider—in order to become a powerful insider himself.

"Having been beaten as a liberal candidate for governor in 1966," wrote Reg Murphy, who was then with the *Atlanta Constitution*, "he had decided that he was going to run a very conservative political campaign in 1970 . . . and he showed up in every town in Georgia at that point, a relentless, hard-working, absolutely charming candidate. . . . He called on everybody except the sheriff, the banker and the newspaperman. He didn't want any support from any of those guys. And that's the way he ran that campaign; he identified the sheriff and the banker and the newspaperman as evil guys and did it very successfully."[1]

Carter's 1970 opponent was popular former Georgia Governor Carl Sanders, a moderate on racial issues who was pro-business. Carter's pollster, Patrick Caddell, found that Sanders was perceived by many Georgia voters as the candidate of the establishment—a "limousine liberal" who had the support of the newspapers, the spokesmen for the Atlanta establishment. "Carter tailored his campaign to exploit these weaknesses," write Professors Numan V. Bartley of the University of Georgia and Hugh D. Graham of the University of Maryland. "A forty-four-year-old peanut farmer from the small south Georgia town of Plains, Carter labeled Sanders 'Cufflinks Carl' and portrayed himself as the common-man candidate. One of Carter's more effective television commercials pictured the door to a country club and contained a message that began: 'This is the door to an exclusive country club, where the big-money boys play cards, drink cocktails and raise money for their candidate: Carl Sanders. People like *us* aren't invited. We're busy working for a living. That's why our votes are going for Jimmy Carter.' . . . Although eschewing outright race-baiting, Carter struck hard at busing, identified himself with the Maddox administration—[Maddox was] unable to succeed himself as governor. . . ."[2]

Carter did not win the first time, but in a runoff he did. "Carter appealed to the same voting groups," write the authors, "which had made Maddox the Democratic nominee for governor in 1966 and for lieutenant governor in 1970 and which had delivered Georgia's electoral vote to Wallace in 1968."[3]

Carter's television commercials tagged Sanders as a Hubert Humphrey liberal and the press was told that Carter would produce evidence so damaging to Sanders he would be forced to withdraw from the race. "What he did give the press," observed Steven Brill, ". . . was a copy of a picture of Sanders and Humphrey on the same platform, which, Carter charged, proved that Sanders was ready to sell out the interests of Georgians to 'ultra-liberals.' On the same day he also accused Sanders of selling out to the 'big unions' by favoring repeal of right-to-work laws."[4]

Later, in his 1976 presidential campaign, Carter would

accept support from "ultra-liberals" and labor unions and would advocate repeal of right-to-work laws even while denying he advocated their retention while governor of Georgia or as a 1970 candidate. He also attacked Brill, as did his presidential campaign aides, contending misquotation and asserting that the entire article "was grossly distorted."[5] Again, as in his 1970 campaign in Georgia, any criticism of Carter by the press could be turned to his advantage by insisting that journalists too are part of the "insiders" who seek to attack the outsider.

Jody Powell, Carter's closest political advisor and press secretary, denied during the presidential primaries Brill's charge that Carter's people had cooked up a racist smear against Sanders. But Atlanta public relations executive Ray Abernathy "firmly backed up the allegation that a 1970 leaflet with racist overtones was prepared by a top Carter official."[6]

Abernathy also contended that the 1970 campaign financed the media campaign of a third candidate in the race, a black lawyer named C. B. King, as a way of taking votes away from Sanders. "I personally prepared all of King's radio ads," Abernathy asserts, "while I was on [Jerry] Rafshoon's payroll and supervised the production. And I helped channel money to the company Rafshoon used to pay for them. . . . I don't know whether Jimmy knew about it, but everyone else did."[7] (Rafshoon is Carter's media advisor and TV expert for the presidential campaign and served the same function in his 1970 campaign.)

Although Rafshoon, Powell and others denied that the 1970 campaign employed a wide range of political dirty tricks, two friendly biographers confirm in substance not only that such tactics had been employed but that Carter himself was aware of what was being done. Howard Norton and Bob Slosser contend that "Carter afterward told some of [his] friends that he 'felt bad' about his actions, and it was known that he had prayed for forgiveness for some of the things that he felt he had had to say and do to get himself elected. . . .

"It was unquestionably a campaign of expediency," they added. "And it worked. Carter confessed it all later—to friends and to the Lord."[8]

In his presidential campaign autobiography, *Why Not the Best?*, Carter glides over the 1970 gubernatorial campaign by stating that "We made an issue of the big shots standing between him [Sanders] and the people."[9] Yet on the next page he makes much of the fact that one of the Atlanta newspapers tagged him in their editorials as a redneck, racist peanut farmer, the very image he cultivated and fostered to win white votes!

His assessment of those attacks by the Atlanta newspapers is highly revealing. For example, he complained that they had a negative effect on "our tentatively-committed, liberal, and idealistic supporters who did not know me personally' and, thus, who might have supported him financially. Further, he contends that the "attacks were actually motivated because the editors recognized me as his [Sanders'] major potential opponent and wanted to destroy me early in the campaign. The attack actually backfired, because it projected me into a position of prominence among the many candidates in the race."[10]

In the end, the powerless outsider had become the powerful insider. The stage was set for another Carter quick change.

NOTES

1. *Newsweek*, July 19, 1976.
2. Numan V. Bartley and Hugh D. Graham, *Southern Politics and the Second Reconstruction* (Baltimore and London: The John Hopkins University Press, 1975). pp. 149-50.
3. *Southern Politics and The Second Reconstruction*, p. 150.
4. "Jimmy Carter's Pathetic Lies," *Harper's*, March 1976.
5. *I'll Never Lie to You*, p. 33.
6. "Deny Carter Dirty Tricks," *Atlanta Constitution*, Feb. 5, 1976.

7. "Jimmy Carter's Pathetic Lies," *Harper's*.
8. *The Miracle of Jimmy Carter*, p. 48.
9. *Why Not the Best?* p. 116.
10. *Why Not the Best?* p. 117.

"Government is a contrivance of human wisdom to provide for human wants."

—Jimmy Carter,
Gubernatorial Inaugural Address
(January 1971)

7

The New South and the New Racism

Jimmy Carter's personality, political style and career can be summarized in one simple phrase: he plans and calculates with precision.

When he was sworn in as governor of Georgia on January 12, 1971, there was every reason to suspect that he already had his sights set on the presidency. "It was an idea that we first started talking about in 1971," Rosalynn Carter recalls. "I think it was when the candidates for the presidency started coming through Georgia. My boys were already men then, and we—my boys and I—decided that Jimmy knew a lot more about things than did these men who were running for President. And about then different people began mentioning to Jimmy that he should run for President."[1]

In matters political, Carter has always respected and heeded his wife. "She has a strong will of her own (which has seemed to get stronger with each passing year),"[2] he observed in his autobiography, complimenting her by saying that "her judgment on political matters is sound. . . ."[3]

When Jimmy Carter gave his inaugural address it served two purposes: it was a radical break from the 1970 campaign rhetoric that got him elected and it was his unofficial declaration of candidacy for the presidency. "At the end of a long campaign," he said a quarter of a way through a routine inaugural speech, "I believe I know our people as well as anyone. Based on this knowledge of Georgians North and South, Rural and Urban, liberal and conservative, I say to you quite frankly that the time for racial discrimination is over. . . . No poor, rural, weak or black person should ever have to bear the additional burden of being deprived of the opportunity of an education, a job or simple justice."[4]

With these statements Carter stunned his supporters and surprised the northern press, which immediately hailed him as one more example of the political leader of the "New South." His supporters, press interpretation to the contrary, were shocked less at the phrase "the time for racial discrimination is over" than at the northern liberal litany of social activisim. "Government is a contrivance of human wisdom to provide for human wants," Carter said. "Men have a right to expect that these wants will be provided by this wisdom."[5]

Significantly, Carter quoted populist-fundamentalist presidential candidate William Jennings Bryan. Whatever his other attributes, Bryan is best remembered in the South for his vigorous defense of fundamentalist religion in the courtroom duel with lawyer Clarence Darrow. In the 1925 Scopes "monkey trial" in Dayton, Tennessee, in which the teaching of evolution in the schools was attacked as contrary to Biblical teaching, Bryan defended the traditions of the Bible and the South. Bryan was the last politician in America, until Carter, to meld politics, religion, and populism as a political theology. In this Bryan failed and Tom Watson failed—as did populism as a political movement earlier in this century—because populism soon degenerated into racial and religious hatred. (This author first made these observations in 1972, in an article entitled "Don't Tread on Me" which appeared in *The New York Times*. (See Appendix 7.)

Carter's 1971 Inaugural put him on the cover of *Time* magazine. His "New South" Administration, in keeping with his maiden speech as governor, was dedicated to the dual proposition of publicly ending the old racism of

Georgia while privately building a political constituency. This coalition, made up of southern liberals, blacks and unions with their political counterparts in the North, was designed to project him into the White House. Thus, his Inaugural was the southern message to the politically liberal financial and communications power centers in the North.

Carter understands, perhaps better than any political leader today, the use and power of spoken and unspoken political messages and gestures. His Inaugural was one such message. Another was given shortly after his Christmas 1972 "public" decision to run for president when, as governor on January 15, 1973, he proclaimed Martin Luther King, Jr., Day in honor of the assassinated black activist leader. An additional message was delivered to southern and northern black and white liberals when a portrait of King was unveiled in the State Capitol on February 17, 1974. We have no way of knowing whether these moves led directly to his 1974 appointment as chairman of the Democratic Campaign Committee, but this post was crucial to gaining the nomination, since it put him in contact with party leaders across the country. We do know that it brought him widespread support among influential black leaders, privately at first and then later publicly. One of those leaders was Andrew Young, former top aide to Dr. Martin Luther King, Jr., now a Georgia Democrat congressman and close advisor to Carter. Another lesser known supporter was white northern liberal Mary King, wife of psychiatrist Peter Bourne, Carter's close friend, advisor and deputy director of his 1976 presidential campaign. Mary King's position with the Carter campaign, her influence over him and her background illuminate a much-neglected side of the Carter campaign and its political goals.

Mary King, a veteran of the southern civil rights movement, first appeared in the news, in 1963, when she spent time in jail for civil rights protests. Later, in 1964, she was communications coordinator for the Student Non-Violent Coordinating Committee (SNCC), a radical black-white activist group in the South. She was also an organizer in Mississippi of the radical, left-wing Freedom Democratic Party. Still later, in 1968, she was a planner of government health programs primarily for blacks for the Office of Economic Opportunity (OEO). King met Carter in 1971; she was the single most powerful influence in persuading him publicly to advocate the multi-billion-dollar National Health Insurance program in his presidential campaign. "Two years ago," Mary King told Kandy Stroud of *The New York Times* before Carter's nomination, "he (Carter) was worried about a comprehensive national health care system. He felt the costs would be prohibitive. I helped him understand the outlandish expenditures under our current system could be absorbed and controlled by national health insurance."[6]

King also claims credit for Carter's support of the Equal Rights Amendment and his stand on abortion. "I helped him understand," King states of Carter, "abortion as an alternative to failed contraception. He had only looked at it as an ethical issue."[7]

King's influence over Carter crystallizes a complex issue while it raises an ethical question. Has the one-time civil rights movement of the 1960s moved from ending legal discrimination in the South and gone beyond such legitimate goals to a program of socialism? And is this what Carter, influenced by liberal and socialist theologians, is really proposing? The ethical issue is whether Carter's presidential campaign, at first under the banner of the "New South," really has become a New Racism. This question needs to be confronted honestly and openly, since his wide range of proposals clearly imply preferential treatment of blacks over whites to "make up for" past sins of racial discrimination and provide preferential treatment based on race.

"From the end of World War II to the inauguration of Richard M. Nixon," write Nathaniel Weyl and William Marina in their scholarly historical work on blacks in America, "American government policy moved steadily for the advocacy of desegregation to support of race blending in schools and neighborhoods. It moved from the principle of equality of rights to that of preferential treatment for Negroes."[8]

We may find the answer to this explosive question by examining the one term of Jimmy Carter as governor of Georgia.

NOTES

1. *The Miracle of Jimmy Carter*, p. 54.
2. *Why Not the Best?* p. 69.
3. *Why Not the Best?* p. 78.
4. Jimmy Carter, Inaugural Address as Governor of Georgia, January 12, 1971.
5. Inaugural Address.
6. "Mary King: A Key Carter 'Brain Truster' From the Beginning," *The New York Times*, July 8, 1976.
7. "Mary King: A Key Carter 'Brain Truster.' "
8. Nathaniel Weyl and Willian Marina, *American Statesmen on Slavery and the Negro* (New Rochelle, N.Y.: Arlington House, 1971), p. 386.

"What Carter did in Georgia is
the best indication of what he'll do in
the White House."

—Hamilton Jordan,
Carter's Campaign Director
(July 19, 1976)

8

Running on Reform and Racism

Jimmy Carter campaigned during the primaries on his "successful" reform of the state "bureaucracy" while he was governor. "When we reorganized the Georgia government," he states, "administrative costs were reduced by more than half, and in some departments substantial reductions in personel billets were made."[1]

However, Rosalynn Carter was asked point blank during her campaigning in North Carolina how many state jobs were eliminated: "Actually, more state jobs were created," she replied.[2] Furthermore, Carter's successor, Governor George Busbee, "has a continuing legislative authorization to reorganize the reorganization."[3]

Carter claimed he saved $50 million a year by economy measures. "The figure is hard to document," writes Al Gordon of the *Congressional Quarterly,* because it represents reduction in projected spending increases rather than actual budget declines. The size of the state budget increased during Carter's administration. A budget analysis done by the U.S. Census Bureau supports Carter's claim to have substantially changed Georgia's spending priorities, with increases in social services and corrections."[4]

All this information was revealed before the primaries. Still, *during* the primaries, Carter would insist that he saved millions and made the state government "more responsive to the needs of the people. I'm proud, really proud of that."[5] Nevertheless, an Associated Press survey made shortly before he was nominated concluded, "the record fails to show savings that Carter says he achieved in Georgia's government.

"The record shows," added the AP report, "that the state budget increased from $1.057 billion in fiscal 1971 to $1.675 billion in fiscal 1975, an increase of 58.5 percent. . . . State employment, exclusive of teachers, rose in Carter's tenure from 34,322 to 42,400, an increase of 24 percent."[6]

Carter's claim that he slashed the number of state agencies from 300 to 22 is also open to challenge because on becoming governor "there were only 66 budgeted agencies before reorganization. The rest were bureaus, committees, councils, and authorities, some of them small with no funds."[7] A similar analysis by *The New York Times* came to much the same conclusion: ". . . he tempered his hard-line attitude on efficiency and compromised on wholesale job cuts," wrote James T. Wooten, "that would have saved millions of dollars and perhaps contributed to a much more efficient government."[8]

His compromise and failure to reduce the state bureaucracy can only be understood by looking at Carter's ambitions to be president. He had told black leaders, for example, "You won't like my [1970] campaign, but you'll be proud of my record as governor."[9] Carter made good on his promise after waging a campaign that appealed to white Georgians. Despite Carter's later claims that he did well among blacks, black Georgia Legislator Julian Bond points out that he won the primary with less than "10 percent of [the black] vote." And the *Congressional Quarterly* concurs: "he conceded the black vote to [Carl] Sanders (who won an estimated 95 percent of it) and concentrated instead on winning the votes of Maddox supporters."

Carter points with pride to the fact that an unprecedented number of blacks were installed in the Georgia state government on various boards and commissions. The number of black employees went from 4,850 to 6,684.[10] His substantial shift of spending priorities, with increases in social services was aimed primarily, but not exclusively, at Georgia's blacks.

It is clear that Carter's failure to cut state spending and jobs was largely because he was looking beyond Georgia to the White House. He had retained white workers while increasing state jobs for blacks, many with large voting constituencies. His record of social spending on behalf of blacks provided the credentials necessary to gain northern liberal support. Doubtless, he believed that he was doing good. But the net effect was to institutionalize the doctrine of racism in reverse.

Carter, it should be said, did not originate this form of New Racism—the sincere belief that government should promote goals, quotas and "compensatory opportunity" for minorities. But the New Racism has grown steadily since the 1965 Civil Rights Act, which specifically forbids such discrimination in reverse. "Favoritism in governmental appointment, promotion, scholarship or entry into any educational institution," observed historians Nathaniel Weyl and William Marina, "on the basis of race is a violation of the Fourteenth Amendment and should be outlawed. Any compensatory advantages given to Americans because of an unfavorable economic, social or educational environment should apply to all persons so handicapped, not merely to those racially so handicapped."[11]

Since these words were written in 1971, government programs for racial quotas have mushroomed and created an explosive resentment among whites and some blacks. Thomas Sowell, a black scholar at the Center for Advanced Study in Behavioral Sciences at Stanford, California, contends, for example, that busing is not a policy but a crusade. Sowell wrote shortly after Carter was nominated that busing and racial quotas are contrary to the U.S. Supreme Court desegregation decision of 1954 and "in many ways go counter to the original concern for insuring individual constitutional rights without regard to color or other group characteristics. . . .

"The grand delusion of contemporary liberals," he adds, "is that they have both the right and the ability to move their fellow creatures around like blocks of wood. . . . It is essentially a denial of other people's humanity. It is a healthy sign that those assigned these subhuman roles have bitterly resented it, though it may ultimately prove a social and political catastrophe if their anger at judicial and bureaucratic heavy-handedness finds a target in blacks as scapegoats."[12]

When Carter was governor of Georgia, he opposed court-ordered busing but institutionalized racial quotas in employment. Now the platform his aides wrote, on which he is running, advocates both busing and quotas, but with language that is misleading. On busing, for example, that platform proposes that: "Mandatory transportation of students beyond their neighborhoods for the purpose of desegregation remain a judicial tool of last resort for the purpose of achieving school desegregation."[13] The same misuse of language, which Thomas Sowell labels lying with language in the name of a noble cause, is seen in the plank advocating racial quotas. The Civil Rights plank affirms the idea of equal opportunity "regardless of race" while repudiating that principle in the very next paragraph: "In reaffirmation of this principle . . . we *pledge vigorous federal programs and policies of compensatory opportunity* to remedy for many Americans the generations of injustice and deprivation and full funding of programs to secure implementation and enforcement of civil rights."[14] (Author's emphasis.)

Jimmy Carter successfully used a program of government reform and racism in reverse to secure the nomination while representing it as something else. "Carter may be more indebted to black support in November," observed *Newsweek* shortly after the Democratic nomination, "than he was in the spring primaries."[15]

Carter's campaign director Hamilton Jordan confirmed this:

"What Carter did in Georgia is the best indication of what he will do in the White House," he said. "You'll see a dramatic attempt to involve blacks in policymaking positions. You'll see blacks in the cabinet."[16]

More than symbolism was apparent when, at the close of the New York Democratic Convention, the benediction was given by Rev. Martin Juther King, Sr., father of the slain civil rights leader. "Surely the Lord," he said, "sent Jimmy Carter to us."[17] The sight of the entire convention holding hands and singing the civil rights hymn, "We Shall Overcome," was proof positive that Jimmy Carter is leading a movement ready to go beyond its original (and, at that time, legitimate) goal of desegregation by advocating a program that is only fully understood by those promoting it!

NOTES

1. *Why Not the Best?* p. 172.
2. "Timing Is Important on Nitty-Gritty," *Goldsboro* (N.C.) *News-Argus,* April 2, 1976.
3. "Carter Has Issued String of Contradictions," *Dallas Times Herald,* March 1, 1976.
4. "Carter: Full Time Campaign Shows Results," *Congressional Quarterly,* November 29, 1975.
5. "Carter's Record as Governor," *The New York Times,* May 17, 1976.
6. "Carter's State Record Disputed," Associated Press dispatch. Reprinted in Richmond *Times-Dispatch,* July 5, 1976.
7. "Carter's Record Disputed."
8. *The New York Times,* May 17, 1976.
9. *The Miracle of Jimmy Carter,* p. 47.
10. *Jimmy Who?* p. 80.
11. *American Statesmen on Slavery and the Negro,* pp. 390-91.
12. "A Black Conservative Dissents." *The New York Times Magazine,* August 8, 1976.
13. National Democratic Platform, 1976, Education Plank, p. 24.

14. National Democratic Platform, 1976, Education Plank, p. 22.
15. "Carter and the Blacks," *Newsweek,* July 19, 1976.
16. "Carter and the Blacks."
17. NBC-TV Convention coverage, July 15, 1976, 11:42 pm EDT.

"Today's irrational nostrums of the New Left can become tomorrow's political policy."

—Jeffrey St. John
Countdown to Chaos: Chicago, August 1968

9

The Counterculture's Coming to Power with Carter

The civil rights movement in the South in the early 1960s, led by Dr. Martin Luther King, Jr., was the mainspring for the radical New Left.

"The New Left was originally a collection of radical student reformers, principally in SDS [Students for a Democratic Society] and SNCC [Student Non-Violent Coordinating Committee]," observed Dr. Edward J. Bacciocco, Jr., of the Hoover Institution at Stanford University. "In the South, SNCC labored for equal rights, economic advantage, political power, and a new order for disenfranchised rural black people. In the North, SDS pledged to dispel materialism, complacency and 'unreasoning anti-communism,' hoping to substitute respect for the human spirit in place of prevailing social values based on individualism and competition. Its goals included altering American political and educational institutions, controlling corporations, ending defense spending, and, with the proceeds, erasing poverty, terminating bigotry, industrializing emerging nations, and founding a powerful New Left movement throughout the United States."[1]

SNCC and SDS failed *as organizations* to achieve these goals. But they produced radical offspring in a series of antiwar marches and protests by students in the 1960s that disrupted universities and ignited incendiary riots in the nation's cities; they successfully staged-managed a violent confrontation with the political "establishment" of the Democratic Party in Chicago in August 1968. (This author has published a study of the radical activity in the 1960s that culminated in the riots at the Democratic National Convention in 1968. The 1969 book is *Countdown to Chaos: Chicago, August 1968, Turning Point in American Politics*. New Left supporters who were *outside* the Democratic Convention in Chicago 1968 were *inside* in the 1972 Miami convention with the antiwar and peace candidate, Senator George McGovern (South Dakota). The McGovern platform contained almost all of the goals articulated earlier as "demands" by the radicals of the New Left and the civil rights movement.

McGovern's major error, however, was his political style. He failed to sell his radical program in an appealing package. It was obvious to most Americans in 1972 that Richard M. Nixon represented the "straight" middle class culture, while the South Dakota Democrat was perceived as the candidate of the radical New Left and the counterculture.

Jimmy Carter's awareness of the "image" necessary to win votes was made apparent in his conversation with Steven Brill in December 1975. In discussing the McGovern campaign, Carter pointed out how McGovern's attack on the Vietnam war brought into his campaign an allegiance of the disaffected: draft-resisters, pot-smokers, hippies, civil rights activists, and peaceniks of wide counterculture motives. While McGovern ran on the issues and stated clearly what he proposed to do with the power of government, Carter discounted this approach as irrelevant, says Brill, "because he knew he'd run on personality."[2]

Apparently Carter's strategy from the inception of his campaign was to appear as a smiling conservative, a Christian, and a member in good standing of the "straight" middle-class culture. Reluctant to sacrifice the support of McGovern's loyal counterculture following, however, he was forming alliances with civil rights activists and counter-culture heroes such as New Left folk singer Bob Dylan, rock singer Gregg Allman, and self-proclaimed drug freak Hunter Thompson. Thompson is star writer of the counterculture magazine *Rolling Stone* which endorsed Carter early in his campaign.

Carter's relationships with former civil rights radicals strengthen this belief. We cited in an earlier chapter, for example, the influential role being played by former communications director of SNCC, Mary King. Another civil rights radical is the former top aide to Dr. Martin Luther King, Jr., Andrew Young, a Democratic Congressman from Georgia. "Andrew Young was told by Carter aides," reported NBC-TV's John Hart during the Democratic Convention, "that he could have any job in a future Carter administration."[3]

The Carter connection with the New Left counterculture and McGovern political constituency was apparently first attempted at the 1972 convention. "Jimmy Carter nominated (Sen. Henry) 'Scoop' Jackson for President in Miami in 1972," asserted black Georgia State Legislator Julian Bond, "then attempted to organize a 'stop-McGovern' movement. When that failed, he approached at least two black Georgia delegates and asked us to mention his name to McGovern as a possible running mate. I did so twice, both before and after Eagleton [Sen. Thomas Eagleton, McGovern's initial choice for running mate], but *now Carter lies and says it wasn't so.*"[4] (Author's emphasis.)

Despite Carter's denial, *Washington Post* political reporters David S. Broder and Jules Witcover contend that Carter aides did approach McGovern's political pollster Patrick Caddell (now Carter's pollster in 1976) with the argument that a southerner would strengthen a McGovern ticket. "Others had been talked to about putting Carter's name forward," they wrote, "including Andrew Young of Atlanta, now a Congressman, and Georgia State Sen. Julian Bond. But nobody took Carter seriously."[5]

In a July 25, 1972, memo, Peter Bourne first raised the

issue of Carter's running in 1976, so certain was Bourne that McGovern was doomed to defeat. "The others didn't know it at the time," wrote Broder and Witcover, "but the same idea had crossed Carter's mind and he had discussed the possibility with his wife, Rosalynn."[6]

It is significant that Peter Bourne was the first to advance a Carter presidential bid. Bourne, Mary King's husband and a close personal friend of Carter, was one of the organizers of Vietnam Veterans Against the War. He was present during the disorders at the 1968 Democratic Convention.[7]

The tactics employed by New Left radicals at the Chicago 1968 riots were identical to those employed by protest groups of the earlier 1960s, including the early civil rights movement lead by Dr. King and aides such as Andrew Young. Young, who did not actively participate in the Chicago disorders, made a revealing statement six months before the riots: "We intend to have the kind of relationship with the violent groups that would say if you can't adopt nonviolence and join us, let us try our way until the first of August *then you can take over with another approach*, but let's not try to mix the two."[8]

A few months later Young was standing on a motel balcony with Dr. King in Memphis, Tenn., when King was shot and killed. The murder unleashed widespread rioting among blacks in the spring of 1968; later, in August, radicals incited disorders at the Democratic National Convention. This was the climax of nearly a decade of an ever-expanding campaign of civil disorders. The purpose from the onset was to use violence or threats of violence to achieve the ultimate objective of taking over the Democratic Party. As this author observed at the time, "Much more dangerous to the Democratic Party's 'Old Politics'—meaning the coalition put together since the days of the New Deal—is the likelihood of a shift to the more extreme political Left to win elections. . . . Helping along in this regard will be those 'New Politics' leaders who have not given up their aim to either smash the party or control it. . . .

"Lacking any firm, intelligent and consistent opposition," we added, "today's irrational nostrums of the New Left can be tomorrow's political policy and dogma. This is the way Nazism came to Germany, first taking the route of the welfare state, then going beyond it to National Socialism."[9]

That book was published in 1969. Three years later the McGovern New Left coalition had taken over—legitimately—by altering its rules and changing its procedures, thus transforming the Democratic Party. Many conservative-to-moderate party members deserted in 1972, contributing to its crushing 1972 defeat at the polls. Jimmy Carter is said to have "healed the wounds" of 1968 and 1972. But the evidence suggests that the healing is on the surface only, with more subtle tactics and strategies rather than any renunciation of the New Left radicalism.

Labor columnist Victor Riesel revealed during the 1972 Miami Democratic National Convention that McGovern had taken into his council United Auto Workers labor leader Leonard Woodcock. "The Dakotan knows, of course," wrote Riesel of McGovern, "that Woodcock is a Fabian Socialist. So are, in varying degrees, many leaders of the UAW, which is directly linked to the Americans for Democratic Action, which is now linked to old leaders of the long-gone American Labor Party and the inner apparatus of Henry Wallace's pro-Communist 1948 Progressive Party.

"Certainly this doesn't insinuate that Woodcock is a Communist. It does mean that for the first time since Henry Wallace's campaign, a national political figure of McGovern's stature has deliberately associated himself with and gone out of his way to use such forces and placed them high in his little-known inner command."[10]

As we shall discover in the following chapters, money and manpower provided by UAW President Leonard Woodcock was crucial in Jimmy Carter's primary campaigns in defeating Alabama Governor George Wallace in the South and in making the former Georgia governor the political surprise of 1976.

NOTES

1. Edward J. Bacniocco, Jr., *The New Left in America, Reform to Revolution 1956-1970* (Stanford, Calif.: Hoover Institution Press, 1974), pp. 229-30.
2. "Jimmy Carter's Pathetic Lies," *Harper's,* March 1976.
3. NBC-TV Convention coverage, New York City, July 12, 1976, 9:30 pm, EDT.
4. Julian Bond, "Why I Don't Support Jimmy Carter," *The Nation,* April 17, 1976.
5. "How Carter Built His Bandwagon," *Washington Post,* May 9, 1976.
6. "How Carter Built His Bandwagon."
7. Elizabeth Churchill Brown, "Piecing Together the Jimmy Carter Puzzle—Appears as Creature of New Left," *Union Leader* (Manchester, N.H.,), August 3, 1976.
8. Quoted from *Christianity* and *Crisis,* Jan. 22, 1968, in *House Divided,* by Lionel Lokos (New Rochelle, N.Y.: Arlington House, 1968), p. 32.
9. Jeffrey St. John, *Countdown to Chaos: Chicago, August 1968, Turning Point in American Politics* (Los Angeles: Nash, 1969), pp. 85, 90.
10. "Unseen Veteran Radicals Creating Social Democratic Party," *The Cincinnati Enquirer,* July 23, 1972.

"We went with Carter to beat Wallace."
—Selina Burch,
Georgia union official
May 27, 1976)

10

The Wallace Vote Without Wallace

The defeat of Alabama Governor George Wallace by Jimmy Carter in the March 9, 1976, Florida presidential primary has been seen as the political slaying of Goliath by David. Without question, the Carter campaign was brilliantly organized; the Wallace organization suffered most from the fact that its candidate was campaigning from a wheel chair.

But the lion's share of the credit for the crucial Carter win in Florida rightfully belongs to a coalition of northern and southern liberals and union bosses like Leonard Woodcock, president of the United Auto Workers (UAW). From the very first, Woodcock's UAW money and manpower was the combination that took Carter from his first caucus victory in Iowa to the Democratic nomination.

In Iowa, for example, Carter showed himself as opposing the federal bureaucracy—like Wallace—while behind the scenes the pro-big-government Woodcock and his organization worked with the locals down to the precinct level. "The United Auto Workers is backing him as a likely winner," commented Joseph Kraft about Carter's "diverse flock of friends" after a swing through Iowa with Carter in January 1976. Yet, Kraft added, "a county official in Burlington said Carter appealed to him because of his opposition to bureaucracy."[1]

In Florida, the same script was followed with brilliant results. UAW manpower and money was the political spearhead of a group called the Labor Coalition. "The coalition was formed," according to an article in the respected *National Journal*, "to coordinate the activities of nine unions to elect as many labor delegates to the Democratic convention as possible and produce a nominee who could unify the party and win the election. . . ."

The article continued, "While the coalition had an impact in several states, its biggest success came in Florida, where it united behind Carter and helped him achieve a crucial breakthrough by beating Wallace in the South."[2]

Also helping out were liberal civil rights activists such as Congressman Andrew Young (Democrat, Georgia) and Georgia State Representative Julian Bond (although Bond later labeled Carter a liar and switched to Morris Udall). Millionaire Max Pavelsky, a California liberal who had backed George McGovern in 1972, helped supply an early and effective advertising campaign.[3] Carter and his backers even persuaded other liberal presidential candidates to refrain from campaigning extensively in Florida so that the field would be left to him and Wallace.

"In the Florida campaign," wrote Leslie Wheeler in her book, *Jimmy Who?*, "Carter was careful not to attack the Wallace 'message'; rather he stressed the fact that he, instead of the Alabama governor, had a real chance to be elected president. He did not want to alienate Wallace supporters; he also wanted to make it possible for Wallace to support him later on. Again, as in New Hampshire, Carter was perceived as a moderate to conservative candidate."[4]

Observers were later puzzled to see Carter collect both the black and the pro-Wallace vote in Florida. Only when he was virtually certain of being nominated did observers understand that his confidence in his triumph over Wallace was well founded—and well financed. The attacks by some liberals on the former Georgia governor served to obscure further the fact of his heavy liberal and union support and only deepened the candidate's mystique that he had a secret, not-easily-discerned formula for political success. AFL-CIO President George Meany remained aloof from Carter during the primaries, and this pose was taken as evidence that unions did not look with favor on his presidential campaign. Even the usually astute *New York Times,* as late as June 1976, was reporting that "the corporate and union political action committees . . . ignored Jimmy Carter during the early months of 1976," and suggested the money only started flowing after his June primary sweeps. "Before May, only the United Automobile Workers and the Amalgamated Clothing Workers had displayed any interest in his candidacy," *The Times* stated.[5]

The depth of the UAW commitment and Carter's appreciation for helping him secure the nomination were finally illustrated when the Carter organization informed the *Christian Science Monitor* labor correspondent that Woodcock was "high on the lists for Secretary of Labor or Secretary of Health, Education and Welfare."[6] Woodcock, three weeks before his consideration by Carter as head of one of the Washington bureaucracies, spoke glowingly of the candidate. "There are things," Woodcock said three days before the June primaries in California, New Jersey and Ohio, "that I have discussed with Governor Carter and find him sympathetic. . . . Mr. Carter has realistic answers to the economic problems this nation faces."[7]

The degree of that "sympathy" was dramatically demonstrated at the Democratic National Convention in New York City. Reporters and delegates alike complained that the convention seemed to be tightly controlled by the Carter camp. In reality, the Woodcock Labor Coalition was in control. "The Labor Coalition won an apparent victory on the floor, . . ." reported *The New York Times,* "when the convention voted to accept a minority report urging that federal statutes be liberalized to give public [union] employees more freedom to participate in politics."[8]

That minority report was the only one adopted by the convention! Southern Wallace delegates, who tried repeatedly to have minority reports adopted on busing, gun control and other conservative issues, were either ignored or crushed. The Alabama governor suffered much the same fate when he presented to the convention the party platform on bureaucracy. While Wallace talked of "getting the government bureaucracy in Washington off the average American's back,"[9] most of the delegates chatted among themselves and generally ignored his remarks. "Perhaps he didn't get a very enthusiastic reception," NBC-TV's David Brinkley shrewdly observed, "because many of the delegates are themselves bureaucrats."[10]

When Jimmy Carter, the anti-Washington and anti-bureaucracy candidate of the presidential primaries, pushed his way through the sea of delegates, smiling in his hour of triumph, almost everyone had forgotten or ignored how and why he had made it.

"Too often," Carter exclaimed in his acceptance speech, "unholy, self-perpetuating alliances have been formed between money and politics, and the average citizen has been held at arm's length."[11]

The long-time political outsider was indeed inside at last.

NOTES

1. "Carter's Success Seems Doubtful," *Long Island Press*, January 14, 1976.
2. "Labor Report," *National Journal*, July 3, 1976.
3. Leslie Wheeler, *Jimmy Who?* (Woodbury, N.Y.: Barron's, 1976), p. 118.
4. Wheeler, *Jimmy Who?* p. 118.
5. "Carter Finally Gets Contributions from Unions and Corporations," *The New York Times*, June 23, 1976.
6. "Woodcock to Get Cabinet Post?" *Atlanta Journal and Constitution*, June 27, 1976.
7. "Carter for Labor, Woodcock Says," *Dayton Journal Herald*, June 5, 1976.
8. "New Labor Group Takes Party Role," *The New York Times*, July 15, 1976.
9. George Wallace, speech, Democratic convention, CBS-TV, July 13, 1976, 9:15 pm EDT.

10. David Brinkley's commentary, NBC-TV, July 13, 1976, 9:38 pm EDT.
11. Carter, Acceptance Speech, Democratic National Convention, July 15, 1976, Transcript in *The New York Times*, July 16, 1976.

"I never make a misleading statement, I never tell a lie, I never betray a trust."

—Jimmy Carter
(April 2, 1976)

11

Primaries of a Thousand Impressions

During his primary campaign Carter was increasingly criticized in the press by his more liberal opponents for being on both sides of an issue.

"Carter tells urban audiences," observed ABC-TV correspondent Sam Donaldson, who has covered Carter from the inception of his campaign, "the farm subsidy program needs changing: specifics to come later. But the impression is left that taxpayer money will be saved. Before farmers, he promises to subsidize their production costs, but does not commit himself to an exact subsidy figure. So there is no direct contradition. It's just that both audiences come away convinced they know where he stands."[1]

Carter's campaign aides complained during the primaries that he was being held to a higher standard than most politicians who also straddle both sides of an issue. However, as Donaldson pointed out, while this is true, "the higher standard by which he's being judged is the one he set himself."[2]

The key to understanding the Carter record is not in his contradictions, but in his reaction to critics who decided to hold him to his self-imposed high standard. In New Hampshire, for example, he told reporters that he found three reasons for the criticism: newsmen not familiar with his record; his surprise political success; and "some slight regional prejudice."[3]

It was this very southern origin and his "outsider" role that he heavily traded on during the primaries. Furthermore, he did not answer the question raised about his contradictory position on the right-to-work laws when campaigning in Massachusetts. Instead, he replied that the criticism "won't hurt me, but I'm afraid it might hurt the country." Then he emphasized, "I want to be the next President of this country. I expect to be the next President. That does not mean I have to take my personal success from personal hatred. . . ."[4]

In these expectations he is certainly sincere, and he resents reporters' questioning his integrity or sincerity. It has always been Carter's style to deflect criticism of his own policies by claiming a higher cause. However, the primary in Wisconsin, a state that went for liberals Eugene McCarthy in 1968 and George McGovern in 1972, was narrowly won by Carter over Arizona Congressman Morris Udall because his appeal was in complete contradiction with the conservative image he had projected in Florida, New Hampshire and other states. *Columbus* (Ohio) *Dispatch* political reporter, George Embrey, described Carter's approach after following him around Wisconsin as the "ability to change his image as a southerner with some obviously conservative background to a leader of liberal politicians in one of the most liberal Democratic states."[5]

Why Carter should react with such hostility to critics of his political switch hitting after violating his own standard remains a mystery. It is a standard that he set after he had demonstrated during his own 1970 gubernatorial campaign in Georgia that he would not be averse to changing his political complexion to blend with a current background or bias. And yet, as a southerner, there is in Carter a touch of "wanting to please" that is characteristic of the region and its people.

"Carter personifies the Democratic party's split," observed Tennessee-born and educated, but long-time

Washington correspondent, Frank van der Linden. "The conservatives who helped him to win primaries in the South and in farm states see him as a conservative who would cut down big government. But he is wooing liberals by promising 'profound changes' in Washington. The party itself is heading in both directions at once. It will be interesting to see how it harmonizes its differences in its platform."[6]

The harsh judgment made of Carter during the primaries may have been unfair, but it was most of all premature. Not until the Democratic Party Platform was adopted in New York and the nation got a close look at his running mate was it possible to make a fair appraisal of whether Carter is a liberal, a moderate or a conservative. His choice of Senator Walter Mondale (Minnesota), an avowed liberal, was said to be one clue. Another was the union-dominated convention, and a platform written to please the liberals and union officials.

Two views from different parts of the nation, one prior to the primary in New Hampshire, the other after the primaries and during the Democratic convention, may provide a fix on Carter politically. "He is a candidate of a thousand impressions," wrote James Wooten of *The New York Times*, prior to New Hampshire, "a liberal, a moderate, a moderate liberal, a conservative moderate, an ambidextrous centrist, a man for all reasons, the peanut farmer who made the best-dressed list."[7]

William Murchison of the *Dallas Morning News* apparently looked at the convention and the party platform and concluded that far from being a liberal or a conservative, Carter had no real "undergirding political philosophy" but like St. Paul was all things to all people as the means to an end. "Thus far," he wrote, "Carter has benefited from a rising conservative tide in the country—a tide generated by discontent with swollen, impersonal bureaucracies, high taxes and national pusillanimity. It is not the liberals who put Carter over, although he does indeed have liberal support, it is the conservatives and moderates."[8]

Perhaps the best index and insight into Carter's political and personal character was not his issue straddling, but how he handled one issue throughout the primaries. It was during the Pennsylvania primary, on April 27, that Carter confronted a single issue that may have turned a spotlight on his character and his true conception of American politics.

NOTES

1. "Evening News with Harry Reasoner," ABC-TV, April 2, 1976.
2. Evening News, April 2, 1976.
3. "Carter Says US Needs an 'Outsider' Like Himself," *Boston Globe*, Feb. 18, 1976.
4. "Carter Deplores Personal Criticisms," *Washington Post*, February 28, 1976.
5. "Carter's Acquisition of Liberal Hue Could Start Wisconsin Bandwagon," *Columbus Dispatch*, April 2, 1976.
6. "Carter, Udall 2 of A Kind," United Features Syndicate, May 20, 1976.
7. "A Broad Range of Impressions," *The New York Times*, Feb. 11, 1976.
8. "Rough Road to November," *Dallas Morning News*, July 15, 1976.

"Jackson said industry has been drawn away from the North by southern states."

—Associated Press,
Pennsylvania Primary Campaign
April 16, 1976

12

Pennsylvania: The Political Gettysburg

It was many years after Abraham Lincoln's "Gettysburg Address" before the nation grasped the strategic importance of the famous Gettysburg battle of July 1863 in that small, sleepy town in south central Pennsylvania. More than a century later, on April 28, 1976, Pennsylvania's presidential primary was a political-economic civil war. It was a strategic turning point for Jimmy Carter, the southerner, in the North. The two principals in this primary were Senator Henry Jackson (Democrat, Washington), backed openly by the powerful AFL-CIO headed by George Meany, and Jimmy Carter, surreptitiously supported by the more liberal and leftist Labor Coalition headed by United Auto Workers President Leonard Woodcock. The public's impression of the primary was that powerful political and union bosses (AFL-CIO) were ganging up on the former Georgia governor, who once again successfully ran against the "insiders" as an "outsider."

But that primary forced Carter to harden his position on issues for the first time, particularly the issue of why industry and jobs had been flowing out of the northern industrial states and into the South. In the primary campaign in Massachusetts—one of a number of New England states hard hit by the southward exodus of textile manufacturers—Carter's allegedly more liberal opponents hit hard at his support of right-to-work laws, sanctioned by Section 14B of the federal Taft-Hartley Labor Act of 1948. At the time of the Massachusetts primary nineteen states had these laws, which have long been loathed by union organizers because of the roadblock they presented in full-scale unionization of those states. This was particularly the case in the Deep South.

Louisiana became the twentieth state with passage of a right-to-work law on July 7, 1976. Eight hours after its passage by the State Senate, on July 8, 1976, Jim Leslie, public relations counsel for the statewide right-to-work campaign in Louisiana, was shot in the back and murdered in a Baton Rouge motel parking lot. Three days later, on NBC-TV's "Meet the Press" on July 11, Jimmy Carter was saying, "I don't have any strong belief on one side or the other and (right-to-work) is something about which I think there is much more of a litmus test on philosophy than there is a deep desire on the part of the labor people, the labor members to pursue."

In Massachusetts, Carter managed to deflect the issue. He dismissed the importance of right-to-work when it was raised by Sen. Birch Bayh (Democrat, Indiana), saying, "I don't think it makes any difference." Bayh shot back that textile and shoe manufacturers unionized in the North went South to right-to-work states like Georgia, and this movement resulted in the loss of tens of thousands of jobs in the North.[1] Rather than answer Bayh, Carter sidestepped by contending that such attacks "won't hurt me, but I am afraid (they) might hurt the country."[2] Continuing to employ the "outsider" image, not influenced by bosses, Carter also stated, "I'm not afraid of criticism because I don't depend on powerful political people to put me into office."[3]

Two weeks before the voting in Pennsylvania, at a closed breakfast meeting of 50 of Atlanta's most influential businessmen, the former Georgia governor asked each of those present to raise $5,000 to aid his cash shortage in the Pennsylvania primary campaign. According to several people who were at that meeting, "the candidate said he had not advocated repeal of Section 14B" and insisted that his position had constantly been "misinterpreted."[4]

Nevertheless, several weeks earlier in Waukesha, Wisconsin, Carter had clearly told a union audience "I think 14B should be repealed" and "if the Congress passes such legislation, *I'd be glad to sign it.*"[5] (Emphasis is author's.) In Pennsylvania, Jackson hit hard at the issue. In reply, Carter accused him of distorting his stand: "(he) constantly hands out erroneous material about me that makes it very difficult, in some instances, for labor union members to support me—right-to-work for instance."[6]

Peter Rubish, a Pennsylvania coal miner and Jackson supporter, confronted Carter on repeal of right-to-work while he was campaigning. "You were the governor," Rubish said somewhat sarcastically. "Geez, you could have done away with it." Carter responded that "what was important was his current position—that as President he would sign a bill repealing Section 14B of the Taft-Hartley Act."[7] Attempting to take the political offensive again, Carter used sarcasm to attack Philadelphia Mayor Frank L. Rizzo, a major supporter of Sen. Jackson. Slyly linking Rizzo and Richard Nixon with the Senator, Carter said, "The last presidential candidate Mr. Rizzo supported was Richard Nixon. I'm glad he doesn't think I'm in the same league."[8]

During the last days of the primary, Carter met with steel executives at Pittsburgh's William Penn Hotel and sought to convince them that he was a friend of business. The very next morning Carter was out at the U.S. Steel Homestead plant promising unionized steel workers to repeal 14B and other legislation favored by unions. "Following his surprising heart-to-heart talk with not unsympathetic titans of industry," observed columnists Roland Evans and Robert Novak on the eve of Carter's Pennsylvania victory, "Carter went to the workers they pay, over the heads of union bosses, and doubly verified the political truth on which his camp is based: political office is more vulnerable than ever to capture by resourceful, imaginative campaigning that exploits the skepticisms and the decay of power in almost all organizations."[9] Beyond his clearly contradictory statements on right to work, Carter's successful campaign in Pennsylvania underscores how a critical issue of importance to both North and South can be blurred and buried, leaving voters as confused as ever.

Richard L. Stout of *The Christian Science Monitor* was perhaps the only reporter covering the primary who grasped the issue. "The controversial right-to-work issue," he wrote, "illustrates the hurdle a Southern governor must leap to reach the White House." Referring to an exchange between Jackson and Carter prior to primary voting, Stout added that it "was an emotion-charged dispute with regional overtones that reminds many Northern workers of textile mills and other plants that have migrated to low-cost areas in the South where often welfare, living costs and wages were below Northern union levels."[10]

A long-time observer of Carter, who first supported and then broke with him over his betrayal of the issue, summed up the issue well. "My personal philosophy and view of Americanism," wrote Ted Oglesby, the Gainesville, Georgia, newspaper columnist, "absolutely prohibits me from accepting the proposition that an American citizen should have to belong to any organization—union or otherwise—in order to hold a job unless he particularly wanted to belong to that organization. By the same token, an American citizen ought to be able to belong to an organization he wants—unions included—without it affecting his job."[11]

Despite Carter's insistence throughout the primaries that the issue was not important to workers, unions, business, North or South, the issue *is* of crucial importance since it comes down to one of *individual free choice versus compulsion.*

NOTES

1. "Carter Attacks Widened by Massachusetts Rivals," *The New York Times*, Feb. 28, 1976.
2. "Carter Deplores Personal Criticisms," *Washington Post*, Feb. 28, 1976.
3. "Mayor White to Contenders: Bury the Hatchet," *Washington Star*, Feb. 28, 1976.
4. "Carter Shifting Stance Again on Right-to-Work Laws?" *Atlanta Constitution*, April 14, 1976.
5. "Carter Gives Stand on the Environment," *Milwaukee Journal*, April 1, 1976 and *Atlanta Constitution*, April 14, 1976.
6. "Carter Raps Jackson," Associated Press, *New York Post*, April 16, 1976.
7. "He's Proud to Do Without Rizzo's Backing," *Philadelphia Inquirer*, April 22, 1976.
8. "He's Proud to Do Without Rizzo's Backing."
9. "Carter Scored Well in Pennsylvania," *Nashville Tennessean*, April 26, 1976.
10. "Right-to-Work Dogs Carter in Pennsylvania," *The Christian Science Monitor*, April 27, 1976.
11. "Carter is wrong on right-to-work," *Gainesville*, (Ga.) *Times*, April 6, 1976.

"His stand on the Right-to-Work issue shows him to be an unblushing liar."
—Reed Larson, National
Right to Work Committee
June 24, 1976

13

The Little Letter and the Big Lie

Shortly after his 1970 gubernatorial victory in Georgia, Jimmy Carter wrote a short, three-sentence letter to Reed Larson of the National Right to Work Committee in Washington. "I stated during my campaign," Carter wrote in reply to Larson who inquired how the new governor stood on Georgia's right-to-work law, "that I was not in favor of doing away with the Right to Work Law, and that is a position I still maintain."[1] (See Appendix 5 for full text.)

Nearly five years to the day after that letter was written, David Broder, political columnist for the *Washington Post,* reported that American unions were unhappy with Carter's position as pledged in the January 1971 letter to Larson. "My commitment to labor leaders in my state in 1970 and since," Carter told Broder, "has been that if they could pass a repeal of right-to-work, I would sign it." "As a matter of fact," Broder observed, "both Carter and Herbert Mabry, the president of the Georgia AFL-CIO, say that repeal of right-to-work is so unthinkable in Georgia that no repeal bill was even introduced in the legislature during Carter's term."[2]

Throughout the presidential primaries, Carter would maintain his consistent inconsistency. "The last two years," Carter told a group of newspaper editors on February 28, 1976, "I've said, to me the right-to-work law is all right the way it is. I don't have any feelings about it, but if it ever passes the Congress without my help, I'll sign it into law. And I told the business community the same thing."[3]

In a national TV interview the following month, Carter again shifted. "When I was running for governor of Georgia," he told a panel of reporters, "I told the labor leaders and also the public that if the Georgia legislature repealed the right-to-work law, that I would be glad to sign it into law. Now, that was when my responsibilities were to Georgia. At that time I did not favor a repeal of 14B, which is a national law.

"Now that I approach the presidency, as a potential President, I've taken the same position, which I think is fairly consistent, although there's some inconsistency there, I admit. But I want everybody to understand that if the Congress passes a repeal of 14B, that I'll be glad to sign it into law."[4]

The inconsistency is larger than Carter admitted. During his 1970 campaign and in 1971 as governor, for example, he said he was *not in favor of doing away with the law.* But five years later, he now says he had told labor leaders during his gubernatorial race and as governor that he *would sign it* if repeal were passed in the state legislature—a bill that no one dared introduce in the first place! In other words, *he did not favor that which he knew would never be introduced or passed.*

Carter's March 14 statement soon gave way to outright advocacy of repeal on March 31 before a union group in a Milwaukee suburb.[5] In fact, the day after this public call for repeal, it was reported he had "reestablished personal contact with labor leader George Meany after more than a year," and as one paper commented, it was "a move that could prove critical to the Georgian's run for the presidential nomination."[6] He had telephoned Meany shortly after his March 14 national TV statement; Meany returned his call on March 22. The outright repeal stance was made public on March 31.[7]

All this may explain the reason behind Carter's gradual shift from a position of no repeal to outright repeal. In fact, we now know that Carter and his campaign aides had been trying for 15 months to "touch base" with the political arm of the AFL-CIO (COPE) and its chairman Alvin Barkan![8]

Apparently when the rival to the AFL-CIO, The Labor Coalition headed by UAW President Woodcock, offered its help, Carter took it while still seeking to woo Meany. He continued to seek Meany's support all through the primaries, while assuring businessmen in Atlanta and Pittsburgh that he was not for repeal.

When Carter finally met with Meany for the first time, on May 14 after his victory in Pennsylvania, he further compromised his credibility when he told reporters, "I did not ask Mr. Meany for his support, nor did he give it."[9] Curiously, no pictures were permitted of the meeting and Carter told reporters later that the meeting was a reestablishment of an old friendship that went back many years. "Intimates of Meany," wrote *Boston Globe* reporter David Nyhan later, "tell a different story. They said [the May 14th] discussion was 'the first extended conversation they've ever had' and that any previous meetings were nothing more than 'handshakes or social occasions.' "[10]

Who does Carter serve, in fact? The people, as he claims, or the union bosses and power interests with the money and influence to win the election? Ever since he set out to capture the Democratic nomination Carter has contended that "ultimate political influence rests not with the power brokers, but with the people."[11] But shortly before his nomination, the Opinion Research Corporation of Princeton, New Jersey, found that "75 percent of the public feels a worker in industry should be able to 'hold a job whether or not he belongs to a union.' "[12]

Reed Larson, of the National Right to Work Committee, contends that Carter risks alienating not only a majority of Americans, but the 82 percent in the South who support voluntary unionism and favor retaining right-to-work laws. "Moreover," observed Larson, "southern voters feel very strongly about their freedom to join or refrain from joining unions; it is unlikely they are going to roll over and play dead while Jimmy Carter makes deals with the bosses of Big Labor which would result in the loss of their freedom.

"There is a matter of honesty. Jimmy Carter has based his entire primary campaign on a pledge never to lie to the voters. Yet, his stand on the right-to-work issue shows him to be an unblushing liar."[18]

NOTES

1. Letter dated January 29, 1971. See Appendix 5 for full text.
2. "An Alliance with Labor," *Washington Post,* February 1, 1976.
3. "Carter Shifting Stance Again on Right-to-Work Laws?" *Atlanta Constitution,* April 14, 1976.
4. "Face the Nation," CBS-TV, Washington, D.C., March 14, 1976.
5. "Carter Gives Stand on Environment," *Milwaukee Journal,* April 1, 1976.
6. "Carter Opposes Work Right Law," *Atlanta Constitution,* April 2, 1976.
7. "Timing, Symbolism Behind Carter's Talk With Meany," *Boston Globe,* May 15, 1976.
8. "Delays Turn Grin to Frown," *Atlanta Constitution,* April 2, 1976.
9. *Boston Globe,* May 15, 1976.
10. *Boston Globe,* May 15, 1976.
11. Carter, Acceptance Speech, Democratic National Convention, July 15, 1976. Transcript printed in *The New York Times,* July 16, 1976.
12. "Public Support for Right to Work At All Time High," Press release, National Right to Work Committee, June 16, 1976.
13. "Jimmy Carter Can't Have It Both Ways," Right to Work News Service, June 24, 1976.

"Carter is trying to build his own labor machine."
—Victor Riesel,
Labor Columnist
(June 22, 1976)

14

Making Peace with the Power Brokers

Jimmy Carter left his meeting with AFL-CIO union chief George Meany in Washington on June 31, 1976, insisting that while he hoped to gain the endorsement of the union giant he "didn't ask for it."[1]

Ten days before Carter's meeting with Meany, however, the respected labor columnist Victor Riesel told a different story. "There are those who say Carter doesn't have to barter with anyone—least of all the AFL-CIO chief George Meany," Riesel wrote. "But those who say so don't include Carter. He and his staff now are concluding almost daily pacts with the labor movement."[2]

The effort of the Carter campaign to secure the backing of powerful special interest union groups included a personal meeting on May 25 at New York's Sheraton Hotel with Jessie Calhoon, president of the National Marine Engineers Beneficial Association. In New York, Carter personally drafted a letter of agreement promising a federal government program to build up the U.S. Merchant Marine in return for union money and manpower. "Calhoon," Riesel reported, "noted that Carter went over every word in the projected letter. He edited it personally. Took out this word, changed that, mused aloud on just how each sentence would constrain him. Finally, they worked it out."[3]

Calhoon made the letter public two days after Carter

won the June 8 Ohio primary.[4] Al H. Chesser, president of the quarter-million-member United Transportation Union made up mostly of railroad workers, concluded a similar agreement with Carter after he promised to use federal government money "to revitalize the railroad industry."[5]

In return for increased billions of federal funds to education, Carter concluded a similar deal with the 1.8-million-member National Educational Association, with its many millions of dollars earmarked for political action and thousands of members who will work for his election. At its Miami Beach convention in June 1976, the NEA endorsed a presidential candidate for the first time in its history.[6] "Carter has been wooing the NEA," reported Riesel, "for almost two years, meeting with them regularly and at least five times since his Iowa victory."[7]

That Iowa victory, as we have seen, belongs to the more radical Labor Coalition headed by UAW President Leonard Woodcock, who controlled from 550 to 600 of the delegates at the Democratic Convention.[8] "Individual leaders of the UAW, from Mr. Woodcock down," wrote Warren Weaver of *The New York Times*," were instrumental in the evolving success of the Carter campaign from the early caucuses and primaries. Some observers attribute the first Carter victory in Iowa in large part to organizing by the UAW union's state leader, Chuck Gifford."[9]

Thus what millions of Americans watched on national television at the July convention was the old politics as usual with a fresh front. "Nineteen seventy-six will not be a year of politics as usual," Carter intoned. "It can be a year of inspiration and hope, and it will be a year of concern, of quiet sober reassessment of our nation's character and purpose—a year when voters have already confounded the experts. And I guarantee you that it will be a year when we give the Government of this country back to the people of this country."[10]

The takeover of Carter by the more leftist-leaning Labor Coalition was a historic turning point for the American trade union movement, although more moderate and less antibusiness than its radical Marxist union brethren in Europe and England. AFL-CIO chief George Meany, who initially stayed aloof from the Carter campaign, got in under the Democratic tent when he belatedly realized that Woodcock's Labor Coalition had stolen a march on him. Because of this factor, Meany endorsed Carter on July 19, 1976, in Washington after staying away from the coronation. "I thank you very, very much," said Carter smiling more broadly than usual. "I appreciate it, and I'm sure when it's all over you will be proud of me."[11]

In the past, the AFL-CIO alone had never been able to achieve what Carter can now provide with the aid of Woodcock's Labor Coalition: *total one-party dominance of the entire federal government*. Carter is a product of the Democratic one-party system in the South (although traditionally conservative). Now, with the one-party control by the liberal-leftist Democrats in the North in union-dominated and union-destroyed cities like New York, we are seeing a meeting and melding of two authoritarian philosophies.

A grim foreboding of the future can be seen in the situation that now prevails in Europe, and especially in England, where the trade unions have virtually strangled the British economy by their total political dominance.

Columnists Rowland Evans and Robert Novak suggested that this is precisely what the Labor Coalition is seeking to create if Carter is elected with the aid of millions in union money and manpower. Evans and Novak pointed out that the Coalition dominated the Democratic Convention and overruled Carter and his staffers when they didn't like a particular proposal. ". . . the Democratic Party has taken long steps," they wrote, "in the past four years—culminating at [the] Democratic Convention—toward the centralized and European party desired by the Labor Coalition and other reformers."[12]

Ironically, the day after Carter had concluded part of his pact with labor leader Calhoon at the Watergate Apartments on May 11, Robert Moss, editor of the Lonn *Economist's* "Foreign Report" gave a remarkable eech in the same city. Moss pointed out that his fellow untrymen in England had not heeded the warnings writ- into the consequences of years of British trade union minance of the political process. "Look into the horror at Britain is becoming. . . . Look at it closely," he told s audience. ". . . Analyze what has happened there, the ks that we now run that in my view could put an end t just to a man's right to choose his job, but to all our litical institutions and traditions, could turn us into a ciety that is communist, with a small c, and could ac- mplish that within a very short span of time.

"Our trade unions," he added, "are not just bargaining er wages or trying to get more men into their ranks, ey are trying to dictate the whole shape of economic d social policy in Britain."[13]

If New York City is not a sufficient warning to the outh and the nation, perhaps Britain is a better forecast what New York City and the nation might be like in e future.

NOTES

1. "AFL-CIO for Carter, Meany Aide Says," *Atlanta Constitution*, July 1, 1976.
2. "Carter Wooing Labor's COPE Into Camp," *Baton Rouge Advocate*, June 22, 1976.
3. "Carter Wooing Labor's COPE Into Camp."
4. "Labor Prepares to Back Carter," *The New York Times*, June 15, 1976.
5. "How Jimmy Carter Rates With Union Leaders," *U.S. News & World Report*, July 5, 1976.
6. "An NEA Endorsement of Carter Would Be a First," *The New York Times*, June 29, 1976.
7. "Carter Woos Labor," *Herald-News* (Fall River, Mass.), June 21, 1976.
8. "New Labor Group Takes Party Role," *The New York Times*, July 15, 1976.
9. "New Labor Group Takes Party Role," *The New York Times*, July 15, 1976.
10. "Carter: 1976 Will Not Be a Year of Politics as Usual,"

U.S. News & World Report, July 26, 1976. Text of a
ceptance speech, Democratic National Convention, Ju
15, 1976.
11. "Carter Ticket," *The New York Times*, June 20, 1976.
12. "Candidate Carter and The Labor Coalition," *Washin
ton Post*, July 19, 1976.
13. "Trade Union Power Brings Britain to the Brink—
Warning to Americans," Robert Moss speech, May 1
1976, Washington, D.C. Reprinted in *Vital Speeches*
the Day, July 1, 1976.

"We are not going to get these changes
by shifting around the same group
of insiders."

—Jimmy Carter,
Boston
(February 17, 1976.)

15

Welcoming the Old Washington Crowd

When Jimmy Carter chose Senator Walter F. Mondale (Minnesota) as his running mate, and announced his choice at the Americana Hotel in New York City on July 15, many Americans expressed surprise. Was not Mondale a 100 percent liberal? Was he not part of the very Washington establishment that Carter, perceived as a conservative with populist overtones, was running against?

"I can tell you that there is a major and fundamental issue taking shape in this election year," Carter told a Boston rally prior to the New Hampshire primary. "That issue is the division between the 'insiders' and the 'outsiders.' I have been accused of being an outsider. I plead guilty. Unfortunately, the vast majority of Americans—like almost everyone in this room—are also outsiders."[1]

Carter had also said, months earlier, that "The people of this country know from bitter experience that we are not going to get these changes merely by shifting around the same group of insiders."[2]

The choice of Mondale was the first clear perception by millions of Americans that, although Carter might be talking like a conservative "outsider," he was willing to act like most Washington establishment liberal "insiders." "I feel a compatibility with Senator Mondale," Carter told a crowded news conference the day he selected, or rather

publicly announced, the protegé of liberal Sen. Hube
Humphrey as vice president. Carter denied that he ha
picked Mondale because he was a liberal and was pushe
by the union bosses.[3]

Two days before the announcement, ABC-TV reporte
Herbert Kaplan had learned that "Labor wants Mondale
Muskie, or Jackson."[4] Moreover, labor columnist Victo
Riesel had reported in his column *two months earlier* tha
Labor's man for the number two spot was Mondale. "It'
all over but the shouting," Riesel wrote in his nationall
syndicated column during the week of May 10, "amon
those forces which want to bargain with Jimmy Carter fo
the vice presidential slot."[5] This information raises som
doubt about the elaborate "screening" and "selection"
process the Carter campaign allegedly conducted betwee
the end of the primaries in June and his announcement o
July 15.

The surprise over the choice of Mondale should hav
been no surprise. The campaign of running against Washington "insiders" was on its face politically preposterous
Former Democrat and governor of Texas John Connally
said as much shortly before Carter's nomination. "Carte
has assumed the burden of the Democrats of the last 25
years," he said, "a party that has passed much of the social legislation that has gotten so many Americans upset
and angry. We should also remember that Mr. Carter will
be leading a Democratic Party that has controlled
Congress 38 out of the last 42 years."[6]

Carter's courting of Washington-based Democratic
leaders should have provided some insight into his
strategy—that his running against Washington may have
had powerful political appeal to the general voter, but it
was not entirely sincere, particularly since Carter had also
been courting for two years the most powerful "insider"
force in the federal city: the trade unions. Furthermore,
the first public indication that Carter has all along been
angling to be an "insider" was when as Georgia governor
he accepted the invitation of the most powerful liberal,
Nelson Rockefeller, to join in the 1972 Trilateral Com-

mission dedicated to finding big government solutions to social problems.[7]

Carter had pursued a political courtship of the Washington insiders for years; the influential and powerful in Washington have always been Carter's quarry through personal contact. According to Vera Glaser, who covers the Washington social scene, "Carter initiated and nurtured some of those personal contacts over a period of years, building on seemingly casual early meetings."[8]

The political payoff came for his campaign when veterans of the John F. Kennedy and Lyndon Johnson regimes began quietly to back Carter, serving as advisors or being mentioned as future appointees and staffers in a Carter Administration. Foundations and liberal think tanks like the Brookings Institution in Washington, headed by Charles Shultze, have been instrumental in priming Carter with liberal jargon and justifications. Another Eastern establishment, the liberal-dominated Council on Foreign Relations, has been drawn on heavily by the former peanut farmer; it is an organization that has penetrated and influenced every national administration since that of Franklin D. Roosevelt. The liberal Committee for Economic Development has also been working with Carter on plans for a government-directed society from Washington. Even the wide network of Washington-based environmental and consumer groups—powerful special-interest groups by themselves—have signed on with the Carter camp. Ralph Nader, for example, conferred with Carter in Plains, Georgia, and Nader's close associate, Mark Green, admitted they see in Carter the possibility of passage of countless laws that have been bottled up in Congress.[9]

Perhaps the most telling evidence of Carter's open welcome to the old Washington crowd is the list of advisors he has taken on. It reads like the Who's Who of the Kennedy-Johnson era—an era that bears the burden and blame for the big bureaucratic government that Carter castigated during his primary campaign. A partial list, (with former positions noted): George Ball, Under-secre-

tary of State; Clark Clifford, Secretary of Defense; Pau
Nitze, Secretary of the Navy; Joseph Califano, Specia
Assistant to the President (LBJ); Theodore Sorenson
Special Assistant to the President (JFK); Richard Gard-
ner, Assistant Secretary of State; Alan Boyd, Secretary o
Transportation; Paul Warnke, Assistant Secretary of De-
fense; Charles Haar, Deputy Secretary of Housing an
Urban Development; William vanden Heuvel, Assistan
Attorney General; Wilbur Cohen, Secretary of Health
Education and Welfare; and Wilbur Ball, Chief, Social Se-
curity Administration.[10]

Walter Mondale, as Carter's choice, was perfectly consistent with the Washington crowd Carter has welcome
into his camp. And Mondale's mentor, Hubert Humphrey
quickly managed to convince Carter to take on Jerry J
Jasinowski, senior economist with the Congressional Join
Economic Committee of which Sen. Humphrey is chairman. Jasinowski is architect of the Humphrey-Hawkin
Full Employment Bill, a massive blueprint for a new gov-
ernment-planning bureaucracy.

The ambitious barefoot boy and "outsider" fro
Plains, Georgia, not far from where Franklin D. Roosevelt had his summer home at Warm Springs, is leading a
coalition of the powerful and the power hungry. The essential idea is to go beyond the New Deal, Fair Deal
New Frontier, and Great Society to the Full Deal!

NOTES

1. Speech, Boston, July 17, 1976. Quoted in *I'll Never Li to You*, p. 167.
2. "Carter Says US Needs an 'Outsider' Like Himself," *Boston Globe*, Feb. 18, 1976.
3. Carter-Mondale News Conference, Americana Hote New York City, July 15, 1976. ABC-TV, 10:00 am EDT.
4. ABC-TV Convention coverage, July 12, 1976, 8:56 pm EDT.
5. "Sen. Mondale for Veep? Meany Looks at Carter Ticket," *Youngstown* (Ohio) *Vindicator*, May 13, 1976.

6. "Meet the Press," NBC-TV, June 13, 1976.
7. "The Ruling Class," *New Times,* June 21, 1976.
8. "War Horses Gallop to Carter." *Richmond Times-Dispatch,* August 1, 1976.
9. "The Waiting for Jimmy Blues." *New York* magazine, July 12, 1976.
10. Sources: *U.S. News & World Report,* July 19, 1976; *The New York Times,* July 27, 1976; *Newsweek,* June 21, 1976.

"It is power that often changes the man and not the man who changes the power."

—Bill Moyers
"Bill Moyers' Journal,"
Public Broadcasting System
(May 6, 1976)

16

Profiles in Power: The Imperial Presidency

Jimmy Carter's nomination, falling as it did so close to the 200th anniversary of the Declaration of Independence, produced a striking and significant contradiction. During his acceptance speech Carter paid tribute to "the moral and philosophical principles" of the Declaration of Independence, even recalling "that the power of government is derived from the consent of the governed."[1]

Carter then praised some Democratic presidents: Franklin D. Roosevelt, Harry S. Truman, John F. Kennedy and Lyndon B. Johnson, telling the delegates, "we are heirs to a great tradition."[2] Unfortunately, that political tradition to which he referred, representing centralized power in the national government, is in complete contradiction to those principles of the Constitution, and to Thomas Jefferson's ideal of the "consent of the governed." Twenty years ago, in 1955, the late John T. Flynn had already noted that, "The American government today and its economic system is radically different from the Republic and the economic system which existed in this country for almost a century and a half. This means nothing less than that we have gone through a political and economic revolution.... The object of these changes has been to torture and ignore the constitutional charter on which our society rests. This was done for the purpose of creating an atmosphere hospitable to the organization and management of a socialist America—but avoiding cautiously the use of the socialist label."[3]

With minor exceptions, our government hewed roughly to the ideals of its founders until 1913. The first major revolutionary change from their original intent occurred that year with the election of Democratic President Woodrow Wilson. The same year saw ratification of two amendments to the Constitution: the Sixteenth, establishing a federal income tax, and the Seventeenth, providing for the direct election of U.S. Senators. "Both Amendments," observed the historian Otto J. Scott, "greatly reduced the influence of the states in the nation's capitol, and enlarged those of the federal government."[4]

Wilson soon inaugurated the Federal Reserve Act to create a central bank. The Act gave the national government centralized control of both the banking industry and the nation's currency. Without the combined economic tools of income tax and control of the currency, Wilson would have found it almost impossible to take the United States into World War I. The dire consequences of Wilson's wartime political and economic policies were seen ultimately in the Great Depression of the 1930s—even though the Federal Reserve Act was supposed to prevent just such an economic collapse.

Franklin D. Roosevelt was swept into the presidency in 1932 on a conservative platform of a balanced budget and decontrol of the private economic system in order to cure the depression; instead he created a powerful political empire of national bureaus, boards and agencies called "the New Deal." ". . . the nation was carried into a completely new terrain in terms of government," observed historian Scott. "It was a revolution conducted during an emergency, at a time when its novelties were assumed, even by some of its authors, to be temporary. By the time it was realized that the nation had been altered beyond the point of reversal, the time for reversal was gone."[5]

In this way one of the world's most open political-economic systems came to an end. In its place was a permanent system guided and regulated by government, sanctioned by the U.S. Congress. From 1913 until the historic resignation of Richard M. Nixon in 1974, a procession of presidents centralized ever more and greater national power and control in the Oval Office, sanctioned by the U.S. Congress, New Deal biographer and historian Dr. Arthur Schlesinger, Jr., recently conceded that liberals like himself played a powerful role in making possible what he called the Imperial Presidency. He acknowledged in 1973 that "the Imperial Presidency grew at the expense of constitutional order. Like the cowbird, it hatched its own eggs and pushed others out of the nest. And, as it overwhelmed the traditional separation of powers in foreign affairs, it began to aspire toward an equivalent centralization of power in the domestic policy.

"We saw in the case of Franklin D. Roosevelt and the New Deal that extraordinary power flowing into the Presidency to meet domestic problems by no means enlarged presidential authority in foreign affairs. But we also saw in the case of FDR and the Second World War and Harry S. Truman and the steel seizure that extraordinary power flowing into the Presidency to meet international problems could easily encourage Presidents to extend their unilateral claims at home."[6]

During the Eisenhower years just such a claim was extended in the creation of new domestic bureaucracies such as the Department of Health, Education and Welfare (HEW). This kind of example of expanding power was rampant in Washington whether a Democrat or a Republican occupied the White House. Now, more than two decades after the creation of HEW, this single national agency consumes the largest percentage of the annual national government budget and exercises unprecedented control over the lives of individual citizens.

During the Eisenhower years, John F. Kennedy and Lyndon B. Johnson rose to prominence and in the 1960s further extended the pattern of expanding presidential power. "At home and abroad," observed Professors Marvin E. Gettleman and David Mermelstein, "the Kennedy and Johnson administrations reveal more similarity than difference. In both cases there is the same commitment to a program of domestic reform in the tradition of Franklin Roosevelt's New Deal. . . . Johnson's plea for a 'Great Society' in the mid-1960s is the most recent manifestation of a continuous tradition of American liberalism, which, when linked to the vast dynamo of American power, has momentous effects on the world."[7]

Johnson's Great Society expanded power both at home and abroad, and in the process contributed to domestic disorders that eventually caused his defeat, along with Nixon's election in 1968. Although Nixon's landslide victory was largely attributable to a conservative campaign, he soon mirrored his liberal predecessors in the conduct of domestic and foreign policy. Watergate, as historian Arthur Schlesinger acknowledges, was the climax of a political trend multiplied over many decades. "The unwarranted and unprecedented expansion of presidential power," he writes, "because it ran through the whole Nixon system, was bound, if repressed at one point, to break at another."[8]

What of the future? Clark Mollenhoff, who served in the Nixon administration and resigned in disgust, contends that another Watergate is possible as long as the President is not held accountable by countervailing power. Further, he believes, "The danger of another Watergate will not end until we eradicate our belief in the divine right of our chief executives and insist on court and congressional mechanisms to force a president to be accountable under all circumstances for the manner in which the laws are administered and enforced."[9]

The explosive growth of the Imperial Presidency since 1913 raises a question that must be seen as the most serious and searching challenge to the political pledges made so far by Jimmy Carter. A clear example is his pledge to reform the national government but *not reduce* its size and power. He is supported in this goal by political leaders of the party that has controlled Congress for 40 years and that bears the major responsibility for creating the Imperial Presidency. Carter is now calling for a series of new programs and for a Democratic majority in Congress that will help him to pass them. "We need a Democratic President," Carter told the convention delegates, "to work in harmony for a change, with mutual respect for change, open change. And next year we are going to have new leadership. You can depend on it."[10] Can this kind of "harmony" between a Congress and President of the same party ensure the necessary check to prevent a future Watergate? Can Carter be depended upon not to abuse power? He is unequivocally on record as advocating vigorous exercise of presidential power.

And, as Bill Moyers told Carter in a TV interview, "If we've learned anything in the last few years, it has been that good intentions in the use of great power is no guarantee that that power will be used wisely. . . . Now after these last ten years, why should someone believe you?" Moyers asked. "They may trust you. They may know that you are sincere and well-intentioned. Yet they know that it is power that often changes the man and not the man who changes the power."[11]

NOTES

1. "1976 Will Not Be a Year of Politics as Usual." Carter's acceptance speech reprinted in *U.S. News & World Report*, July 26, 1976.
2. "1976 Will Not Be a Year of Politics as Usual."
3. John T. Flynn, *The Decline of the American Republic* (New York: Devin-Adair, 1955), p. 152.
4. Otto J. Scott, *The Professional—A Biography of J.B. Saunders* (New York: Atheneum, 1976), p. 41.
5. Scott, *The Professional,* p. 167.
6. Arthur M. Schlesinger, Jr., *The Imperial Presidency* (Boston: Houghton Mifflin, 1973), p. 208.
7. Marvin E. Gettleman and David Mermelstein, Eds., *The Great Society Reader—The Failure of American Liberalism* (New York: Vintage Books-Random House, 1967), p. 11.

8. Schlesinger, *The Imperial Presidency*, p. 275.
9. Clark Mollenhoff, *Game Plan for Disaster* (New York: W. W. Norton, 1976), p. 11.
10. "1976 Will Not Be a Year of Politics as Usual."
11. Bill Moyers' "Journal," PBS broadcast, May 6, 1976.

"He won't be much different from
the Democrats of the New Deal."
—Dan Cordtz,
Economics Editor, ABC-TV
(July 14, 1976)

17

Platform Comparisons: McGovern '72 Carter '76

Former Texas Governor John Connally was asked by a reporter shortly after Carter's nomination how he viewed the former Georgia governor. "Jimmy Carter is just Southern fried George McGovern, that's all," he replied.[1]

A list of former McGovern supporters and aides active in the 1976 Carter campaign is evidence to support Connally's evaluation. On the list, for example, are Maurice Dees, fund raiser for McGovern in 1972, who in 1976 raised sizable sums for Carter; Patrick Caddell, McGovern's pollster in 1972, who became Carter's pollster in 1976; Frank Mankiewicz, McGovern's campaign director, who became a key advisor to Carter; Lester Thurow, an MIT economist and a McGovern advisor in 1972, who became a Carter advisor on economics; and Chris Brown, McGovern cochairman in Seattle, who became Carter's New England coordinator in 1976.

A comparison of the 1972 McGovern platform and the platform drafted by Carter's campaign aides reflects, with but a few exceptions, the 1972 proposals of McGovern, which millions of voters regarded as radical only four years ago.

But only one member of the platform committee voted against its adoption, and he was defeated soundly. Louisiana State Representative Louis "Woody" Jenkins sought unsuccessfully to have the Carter platform modified with a series of more conservative proposals. He also failed at the convention to obtain a roll-call vote on the platform, which passed by a voice vote. "The Carter platform," observed Jenkins, "is a frightful document, perhaps even further to the left than the one drafted by the McGovern crowd in 1972."[2]

Both the 1972 and the 1976 platforms call for national health insurance, a government-guaranteed annual income, amnesty for draft dodgers and deserters, abortion, busing, racial quotas, greater regulation of business, repeal of right-to-work laws, and larger national aid to education. "About the best that can be said for the platform of 1976," wrote columnist James J. Kilpatrick, "is it is 24 pages shorter than the platform in 1972. This time the tone is not so shrill, but the party still beats the same old leftist drums. The industrious carpenters have put together 200 liberal planks. One is hard put to find a conservative splinter."[3]

Whereas the Carter platform parallels McGovern's in substance, the real and radical change is in the use of language. On income redistribution, for example, both platforms were committed to using the full force of the national government to take from the "have's" and give to the "have not's."

- *McGovern 1972:* "We must restructure the social, political, and economic relationships throughout the entire society in order to ensure the equitable distribution of wealth and power."[4]
- *Carter 1976:* "We do pledge a government that will be committed to a fairer distribution of wealth, income and power."[5]

The Carter platform does advance a number of proposals not set forth by McGovern in 1972: national economic planning under an act known as the Humphrey-Hawkins Bill; political control of the Federal Reserve System (independent of direct political control in the past); a federal office of citizen advocacy; a national takeover of welfare from the states and cities; and a domestic council on wage and price controls. Combined with the McGovern proposals of 1972, the Carter platform goes well beyond the concepts millions of Americans rejected in that year.

What of the costs? Shortly after the platform's adoption in Washington in June 1976, CBS News gave it a price tag of *$30 billion.*[6] The American Legislative Exchange Council, a federation of state legislators based in Washington, offered a detailed analysis of the costs of the Carter platform. *"It is estimated,"* wrote the organization to its members, *"that the proposed programs and provisions in the 1976 National Democratic Platform will require a $100-$125 billion annual increase in the Federal budget.* This is a 25% increase over the current $400 billion annual Federal budget. The breakdown of estimated increases is as follows: mandatory universal national health insurance (requiring a 4½% tax increase for every employee), + $80-$100 billion; national economic planning (Humphrey-Hawkins bill), + $16-$34 billion; a guaranteed annual income (Family Assistance Plan), which would double the current caseload, +$11 billion; nationwide child care programs (Mondale-Brademas bill) +$5-$10 billion; increased bureaucracy and miscellaneous programs, +$5 billion. (Savings from further defense cuts, plus increased revenue to the Federal government by cutting investment tax deductions, would total an estimated $17-$35 billion, bringing the total estimated increases of $117-160 billion down to $100-$125 billion a year.)"[7]

The above estimates exceed the price tag put on McGovern's proposals in 1972. Nevertheless, the 1976 platform claims "The initiatives we propose do not require larger bureaucracy. They do require committed government."[8]

The estimated costs do not include the price of campaign promises made by Carter to various union leaders for new programs and increased national spending for education, and for rebuilding the nation's railroads and the American Maritime fleet.

One can only speculate why Carter tried to disavow political paternity of sections of the platform. "I didn't have any input," he said during a news conference when announcing Sen. Walter Mondale as his running mate." Nor did I try and dominate the platform."[9] But *New York Times* reporter David Rosenbaum, who covered the platform hearings in Washington, told a different story. "Time and again," he wrote, "Mr. Carter's spokesman, Stuart Eizenstat, took the microphone to urge the delegates to delete 'buzz words,' to 'avoid emotional issues' and to eschew 'purple language that is going to give the Republicans pot shots.' "[10] John Chancellor of NBC News concluded that the platform was in fact Carter's child. "It's Jimmy Carter's platform," he said, "whether or not he denies he had a hand in it."[11]

The truly radical nature of the Carter platform and campaign was stripped of its fuzzy phraseology by Socialist Michael Harrington. In 1968 Harrington predicted that "The country has no choice but to have some larger ideas and take them seriously.... Liberalism as it has been known for these three decades cannot respond to the challenge unless it moves sharply to the democratic left."[12] With the radicalization of the Democratic Party after the 1968 riots, Harrington wrote that supporters on the liberal and American left were pushing for "a truly radical restructuring of the society," and that they should seek the "transformation of the Democratic party."[13]

Of the 1976 Carter platform Harrington wrote, "If there were ever any doubt about the subject—and frankly there was not—the 1976 Democratic Party platform shows why the Democratic nominee must be elected in November. The Democrats have taken a progressive stand on critical domestic issues.... For these reasons, among many others, the democratic Left should work enthusiastically for the Democratic ticket during this campaign."[14]

Dan Cordtz, former staffer on the business publication *Fortune*, and now ABC-TV economics editor, was less enthuastic in his appraisal of the Carter platform. "He won't be much different from the Democrats of the New Deal," he said of Carter. "He will probably be a big spender."[15]

Frank Reynolds, on the same network, provided perhaps the most telling comment when he offered an evaluation of Carter's acceptance speech: "His speech might have been written by George McGovern who said the same thing four years ago."[16]

NOTES

1. "Connally Brands Jimmy As Just a McCarter," *New York Daily News,* July 29, 1976.
2. Frank van der Linden, Interview with Rep. Jenkins at New York City convention, *Nashville Banner,* July 12, 1976.
3. "Democratic Platform Called Another Bad Joke," *Raleigh (N.C.) News and Observer,* July 18, 1976.
4. The National Democratic Platform 1972. Text reprinted in *Congressional Quarterly,* July 15, 1972, p. 1730.
5. The National Democratic Platform 1976, Preamble, p. ii.
6. CBS-TV Evening News with Walter Cronkite, Leslie Stahl report, June 15, 1976.
7. American Legislative Exchange Council, 1976 National Democratic Platform Fact Sheet, July 14, 1976, p. 4.
8. The National Democratic Platform 1976, "Government and Human Needs," p. 18.
9. Carter-Mondale press conference, Americana Hotel, New York City. CBS-TV, July 15, 1976, 10:31 am, EDT.
10. "Democrats Adopt a Platform Aimed at Uniting Party," *The New York Times,* June 16, 1976.
11. NBC-TV Convention coverage, New York City, July 13, 1976, 8:44 pm, EDT.
12. Michael Harrington, *Toward a Democratic Left,* (New York: Macmillan, 1968).
13. Michael Harrington, "Don't Form a Fourth Party; Form a New First Party," *The New York Times Magazine,* Sept. 13, 1970.
14. "Carter and the Platform: Room for the Left," *Newslet-*

ter of the Democratic Left, June 16, 1976, Vol. IV, No. 6.
15. ABC-TV Evening News, July 13, 1976.
16. ABC-TV Evening News, July 16, 1976.

"Planning leads to dictatorship."
—Dr. F. A. Hayek,
1974 Nobel Prize Winner

18

The New Bureaucracy: The Old Tyranny

Jim Killilea, a Massachusetts delegate, uttered the most profound observation of the entire Democratic National Convention. "A politician is a magician," he said, "but a magician uses his hands to deceive people. A politician uses his mouth."[1]

Jimmy Carter is a super politician-magician. Not only did he manage to unite the faction-ridden party of Roosevelt, Truman, Kennedy and Johnson, but he persuaded millions of Americans that the past was facing the future with new ideas. "Our people are searching for new voices and new ideas and new leaders," he told the convention.[2]

The fact remains that Carter is marching squarely into the future looking backwards. Nowhere is this better illustrated than in the party platform. "Of special importance," asserts the plank in the platform on the economy, "is the need for national economic planning capability. This planning capability should provide roles for Congress and the Executive as equal partners in the process and provide for full participation by the private sector, and state and local government. Government must plan ahead like any business, and this type of planning can be implemented without the creation of a new bureaucracy but rather through the well-defined use of existing bodies and techniques."[3]

An obvious contradiction is being evaded by the authors of the platform. When the private sector of business plans, it is a *voluntary act*. When government gets into economic planning it is backed with the *full and coercive power of government*. A second fact they conveniently ignore is that national economic planning was tried and failed during FDR's New Deal. In 1943, for example, Congress discovered that it had provided funds for the National Resources Planning Board, busily building a blueprint for a government planned and regimented economy when World War II came to an end.[4] Ironically, the abolition of the planning board by Congress in 1943 came in the middle of a great war against totalitarian regimes that had made economic planning a central pillar of their authoritarian governments.

The current Democrat platform proposals for national economic planning are supported by a long list of liberals and leftists, some of whose careers go back to the FDR New Deal: Leonard Woodcock, president of the United Auto Workers; Abram Chayes of Harvard University; Roy Wilkens of the NAACP; Coretta King, widow of Dr. Martin Luther King, Jr.; and Vernon E. Jordan of the Urban League.[5]

All of the above have been active in the Carter campaign, along with Jerry J. Jasinowski, senior economist with the Congressional Joint Economic Committee of which Senator Hubert H. Humphrey is chairman. Jasinowski was the drafter of "The Humphrey-Hawkins Full Employment and Balanced Growth Act of 1976." While Humphrey and the Democratic Platform are busy asserting that the bill is a means to achieve full employment, we shall see it unmasked as a massive blueprint for further controlling, regulating and regimenting the private economic system from Washington.

In 1975 when Humphrey and Senator Jacob Javits (Republican, New York) first introduced this measure they named it "The Balanced Growth and Economic Planning Act of 1975." It failed to receive substantial support in either House of the Congress, despite the widespread publicity lavished on it. Many lawmakers were apparently hesitant to approve it because of the radical word "planning," invoking images of the government-command economics under Communism, Fascism and Nazism. Predictably, in 1976 Humphrey changed the name of the bill to "The Full Employment and Balanced Growth Act of 1976." But only the name was changed, it seems; in an interview in May 1976, Humphrey admitted that the bill is a "general economic policy bill" and not a "jobs bill," as it was sold to the country. "Not only is this the correct thing to do on its merits," Humphrey insisted, "but it significantly strengthens the political appeal of the bill."[6]

Despite the Democrats' denial that no new bureaucracy would be needed, at least one advocate of planning has a different opinion. Myron Sharpe, editor of *Challenge* magazine, writes, "It will take perhaps a staff of 500 people to do the work and will cost possibly $50,000,000 a year. The plan will analyze and set general objectives for the allocation of resources, labor, and capital to specific sectors of the economy; and will set general objectives for the goods and services produced by those sectors."[7]

Ten days after the Democratic Convention adopted that planning plank, Jimmy Carter stood in front of top corporation heads at New York's exclusive "21" restaurant and promised: "I will be a friend to business."[8] He also asserted, "I've never had a goal for government to dominate business."[9] Thomas Carroll, sophisticated chairman of the board of Lever Brothers, recognized a soft-soap job when he saw it. "I thought this was a velvet performance of an iron-cast man;" he said later to syndicated columnist John Lofton, "I learned more about the man than I did about the issue."[10]

The fact remains that Carter has been an advocate of government planning for most of his political career. When serving on his local county planning board, he recalls, "We learned as planners to assume the role of servants and not masters, and we also learned to combine practical implementation plans with theoretical concepts of planning."[11]

The historical evidence regarding planning contradicts

Carter. Planning by governments has inevitably led to mastery by the few over the many. Hans Willgerodt, professor of economics at the University of Cologne, West Germany, provides a depressing history of the failure of government-imposed planning. "In the twenty years prior to the West German economic reforms of 1948," he writes, "Germany experimented with a number of approaches to central planning and government intervention in the economy. Beginning in the final days of the Weimar Republic, the German economy was gradually transformed from an imperfect market economy into a centrally-administered economy in a totalitarian state."[12]

Another highly respected commentator on the controlled economy is Friedrich A. Hayek, 1974 winner of the Nobel Prize in Economics. In 1944, after witnessing the rise of Nazism, Fascism and Communism through control of the economy, Dr. Hayek was moved to write a book that has become a classic, *The Road to Serfdom.* In *The Road to Serfdom* the international economist contends that Nazism and Fascism were the direct outgrowth of socialist beliefs embraced by political leaders who believed the system could remain democratic. "Planning leads to dictatorship," he wrote in 1944 when the West was still fighting Nazism, "because dictatorship is the most effective instrument of coercion and the enforcement of ideals and, as such, essential if central planning on a large scale is to be possible."[13]

In a chilling note on what could happen here, Dr. Hayek adds, "Hitler did not have to destroy democracy; he merely took advantage of the decay of democracy and at the critical moment obtained the support of many to whom, though they detested Hitler, he yet seemed the only man strong enough to get things done."[14]

NOTES

1. ABC-TV Convention coverage, New York City, July 14, 1976, 9:46 pm EDT.
2. Carter acceptance speech, transcript printed in *U.S. News & World Report,* July 26, 1976.

3. The National Democratic Platform 1976, "Modernizing Economic Policy," p.3.
4. John T. Flynn, *As We Go Marching* (New York: Free Life Editions, 1973), p. 183.
5. *Planning Newsletter,* published by the Initiative Committee for National Economic Planning, Inc., January/February 1976, No. 1.
6. Interview with Sen. Hubert Humphrey, *Challenge* magazine, May/June 1976.
7. "The Planning Bill," in *The Politics of Planning: A Review and Critique of Centralized Economic Planning* (San Francisco, Institute for Contemporary Studies, 1976).
8. "Carter Says He Is Friend of Business," Associated Press dispatch in *The Raleigh* (N.C.) *Times,* July 23, 1976.
9. "Carter Assures Business of Caution on Taxes," *The Washington Star,* July 23, 1976.
10. "Carter's Tax Overhaul," *Manchester* (N.H.) *Union Leader,* August 3, 1976.
11. Jimmy Carter, *Why Not the Best?* p. 112.
12. "Planning in West Germany: The Social Market Economy," in *The Politics of Planning,* p. 1.
13. Friedrich A. Hayek, *The Road to Serfdom* (Chicago: Phoenix Books, The University of Chicago Press, 1944), p. 70.
14. Hayek, *The Road to Serfdom,* p. 68.

"We are all too prone to support any cause with a 'noble' label. We suffer from the tyranny of idealism."

—John V. Van Sickle

Freedom in Jeopardy

19

The Business of Bureaucratic Power

Jimmy Carter addressed the U.S. Conference of Mayors in Milwaukee two weeks after his nomination, telling his audience, "We can no longer afford the price of [government] red tape."[1] The next day in Washington his chief economic advisor, Lawrence R. Klein, told a Congressional committee that a $10- to $15-billion program of tax cuts and government spending programs would be needed in 1978 to correct "the underperformance of the economy."[2] Klein went on to propose the possible use of an "incomes policy," which boil down to government wage and price controls.[3] These proposals would, without question, increase government red tape.

This citation is *not* just one more example of Carter's contradictions. Instead, it points up one very important *consistency*: reliance on the vigorous use of government power. One needs to listen closely to Carter to grasp his real meaning. For example, his comment "We can no longer afford the price of red tape" was followed up by a pledge to the mayors that his administration's urban program "would offer greater federal aid for low-cost housing, fewer restrictions on the use of federal funds for urban transit, and endorsement of anti-recession measures to bring down the rate of unemployment among adults and teenagers."[4] Obviously Carter and his chief economic advisor are advocating *not* less bureaucracy, but a reorganization of governmental powers and a redirection toward a socialist-type economy. In this regard, *Business Week* magazine called Carter "a fairly typical Democrat" while pointing out that "he opposses inefficient government more than big government."[5]

In short, he is committed to the business of using bureaucratic government power. This history and evidence that government policy brings about the exact opposite of the stated goal appears unimportant to Carter. Like most American political leaders of his generation, he is confident that his judgment—and that of his advisors—is wiser, better and more sophisticated than that of the average American making individual decisions in an open competitive market. He may repeatedly speak of the "sound judgment" of the American people, but he fails to recognize that his "vigorous" use of government power would prevent the free exercise of that judgment.

It is clear that Carter suffers from the tyranny of idealism, an affliction identified by Professor John V. Van Sickle. "We are all too prone to support any cause with a 'noble' label," said Van Sickle. "We suffer from the tyranny of idealism. We tend to forget that good intentions are not enough, that there are seldom quick and easy solutions for ancient evils. We are impatient with the seemingly slow pace at which the voluntary forces in a free society proceed against these evils. Our very idealism blinds us to the virtues of the market and the shortcomings of state."[6]

That Carter has little confidence in the concept of individual free choice in the democratic and decentralized voluntary system of the private marketplace is vividly illustrated by his fervent support of two issues: government consumer protection and national health insurance. These government programs, when stripped of rationalization, are a clear pre-emption by government of all choice, replacing a multitude of individual choices with an enforced standard dictated by an elite.

It was not surprising that Carter joined forces with consumer crusader Ralph Nader shortly after his nomination. Nader praised the former Georgia governor's stand on consumer protection, health, energy, economics, and the encouragement of citizen initiative, while implying that the Ford administration had failed in these areas.[7] Each of these areas has undergone extensive control by government in the last decade, swelling the national bureaucracy and budget. These areas also represent a powerful political coalition that Nader is leading to gain greater national-state power over the private sector.

Carter's joining forces with Nader and his support of a national consumer protection agency is significant in two ways. First, it was the most solid evidence that Carter had shed his anti-Washington and anti-bureaucracy image of the primaries. Second, it confirmed an April 2, 1976, analysis provided by *Wall Street Journal* reporter James P. Gannon that, despite Carter's anti-Washington rhetoric he is "a Big Government man."

"A government run by a President Carter," Gannon wrote, "wouldn't be smaller or less expensive than today's. It would not be a do-less, but a do-more government. Washington's organization chart might be drastically redrawn . . . while the bureaucracy would be working overtime to carry out Mr. Carter's big ideas: a sweeping soak-the-rich tax overhaul; a new national welfare system; a comprehensive health care program; an enlarged federal education plan; a gun-registration plan; and a jobs-for-youth program."[8]

If all of this is reminiscent of Franklin Roosevelt's New Deal philosophy, so is Carter's support of Nader's Consumer Protection Agency. Richard J. Leighton, a Washington attorney, pointed out in a 1973 study published by the American Bar Association, that the consumer crusade by government goes back to the Twenties and Thirties. In the FDR New Deal under the National Recovery Administration, later declared unconstitutional by the U.S. Supreme Court, a Consumer Advisory Board was set up. "Despite the great expectations," Leighton wrote in his extensive study, "the New Deal consumer organizations proved to be unsuccessful, even in the minds of consumer activists.

"But this great experiment did contribute immensely, in its own way, to the movement in the 1960s and 1970s for a major federal consumer advocacy unit. Much of the argumentation today in favor of similar consumer advocacy units is merely a replay of what was said in the 1930s."[9]

Economist and author Mary Bennett Peterson pointed out, moreover, that prior to the FDR New Deal the greatest government effort at consumer protection was Prohibition. "Prohibition and its long-lingering aftermath suggest," she wrote in her book *The Regulated Consumer*, "that regulation of any single industry is not easy, that business regulation is indeed people regulation—i.e., consumer regulation. Lawful and 'moral' Prohibition produced not the intended 'era of clear thinking and clean living' but an era of lawlessness and moral laxness. The 'protected' consumer lost again."[10]

Carter singled out the failure of Prohibition in a January 1976 interview when talking about legislating the moral conduct of individuals. "But society just didn't accept it," he said of Prohibition, "and wouldn't accept it now. So when you go too far in trying to legislate morals, people react against it, and the law becomes ineffective."[11]

Carter recognizes that Prohibition failed, but now he proposes to apply the very principles and government power that produced those disastrous consequences to nearly all other phases of the private marketplace and individual choice. Ironically, in the week that he and Nader met in Plains, Georgia, and came to an agreement, a national news magazine reported on "The Bureaucracy Explosion" as a key issue in the 1976 campaign, citing the growing anger and resentment of millions of Americans toward the Washington bureaucracy. "People are complaining," observed the magazine, "about unethical antics of Congressmen and ever-upward spending by federal agencies.

"Over and over, the word is being passed to politicians

that people are fed up with the bloated bureaucracy."[12]

Instead of responding to this massive discontent of Americans with a program of genuine reform and repeal, Carter appears to be responding to special interest groups like Nader's and others who want more, not less, national bureaucracy. Carter's proposal for a national health insurance plan, for example, is not the outgrowth of a demand by a majority of Americans; it is demanded by a small minority headed by an advisor, Mary King. Carter initially had misgivings about its costs, but now favors it. A national health insurance program would, in whatever form, create a new bureaucracy and power elite and send costs soaring. This is precisely what happened when the Great Society Medicare program was created in the 1960s. At that time, the program was based on the belief that it would be cheaper than private medicine; after the program was in motion costs began to skyrocket, waste set in and duplication and scandal soon followed. "A good part of the cost," wrote Marvin Edwards, then editor of *Private Practice* magazine, "was in administrative expense for maintaining the Medicare bureaucracy."[13]

Edwards pointed out that the idea of a national health insurance has been proposed, debated and tried over the last 300 years, all the way back to Queen Elizabeth I of England. He also pointed out that whenever such a plan has been tried, whether in the past or in the present by other governments outside the United States, it has created for the individual consumers of medical services exactly the opposite intended by its advocates. Citing the skyrocketing costs for socialist government-directed medicine in Sweden and other cradle-to-the grave schemes, he pointed out that it has produced one of the most heavily taxed group of citizens in the world. "Sweden's experience is not unique." Edwards stated, ". . . The evidence in other nations with national health insurance and broad-scale welfare programs indicates that a similar prospect is in store for the United States if this country pursues similar policies."[14]

This warning was issued in 1972 when a full accounting of the costs of the Democratic Lyndon Johnson's programs, like Medicare, could not be fully measured. But now they can be. Ten years after The Great Society was launched in 1964, $860 billion had been spent. "Now many of the Great Society programs are being judged harshly," observed a national magazine a year before the 1976 presidential election. "Some points by critics: Poverty is still rampant. Disadvantaged children, despite the billions poured into education, have shown little progress in learning. And the cities, though free of the rioting of the 1960s, are beset by crime and decaying services.

"... A look at the record," the magazine adds, "of the past decade leaves the lingering uncertainty of whether planning in Washington, even if supported by billions and billions of dollars, can ever really cure the nation's ills."[15]

NOTES

1. "Carter Pledges Less Red Tape." *The News and Observer,* Raleigh, N.C., June 30, 1976.
2. "Need Seen to Stimulate '78 Economy." *Washington Post,* July 29, 1976.
3. "Carter's Top Economic Aide Urges $10-$15 Billion in Stimulus." *Baltimore Sun,* July 29, 1976.
4. *The News and Observer,* Raleigh, N.C., June 30, 1976.
5. "Jimmy Carter on Economics," *Business Week,* May 3, 1976.
6. John V. Van Sickle, *Freedom in Jeopardy: The Tyranny of Idealism* (Ottawa, Ill.: Green Hill Publishers, 1969) p. 174.
7. "Nader Likes Carter's Position on Consumer Issues." *Chicago Sun-Times,* August 8, 1976.
8. "The Activist, Carter Despite Image of 'Outsider' Favors Do-More Government," *Wall Street Journal,* April 2, 1976.
9. "Consumer Protection Agency Proposals: The Origin of The Species," *Administrative Law Review* (American Bar Association), 1973, p. 275.
10. *The Regulated Consumer* (Ottawa, Ill.: Green Hill Publishers, 1976) p. 35.

11. *The* (Boston) *Real Paper,* Feb. 25, 1976, story by Andy Merton, as quoted in *I'll Never Lie to You,* p. 99.
12. "The Bureaucracy Explosion—Key Campaign Issue," *U.S. News and World Report,* August 16, 1976.
13. Marvin H. Edwards, *Hazardous to Your Health* (New Rochelle, N.Y.: Arlington House, 1972), p. 62.
14. *Hazardous to Your Health,* p. 90.
15. "A Decade of the Great Society—Success or Failure?" *U.S. News and World Report,* June 9, 1975.

"We are going to reverse the trend that has destroyed the American family."

—Jimmy Carter
Manchester, N.H.
(August 3, 1976)

20

Education:
A Clue to Character

No single issue can provide a more accurate clue to the true character of a political candidate than the candidate's view of education. Education has traditionally been the mainstay of America's proud individualism, the key to economic independence and cultural understanding, and a means for passing on to the next generation the moral values accepted by the society. "No institution," observes historian Anne Husted Burleigh, "plays a more central role in the life of the American family than the public school. Perhaps even more than the church the public school provides the context in which people make the major decisions of their lives."[1]

In *Why Not the Best?* Jimmy Carter pays tribute to the influence of his own school and teacher in Plains, Georgia. "My life was heavily influenced," he writes, "by our school superintendent, Miss Julia Coleman, who encouraged me to learn about music, art, and especially literature."[2] Carter comes from a close and tightly knit family of which he was the first to achieve a college education. This experience may account for his apparent failure to perceive the many negative influences modern public education has had on the family structure in the last half century. "One of the most vital functions of the family," writes educator-historian George C. Roche, "is the education of children. However astonishing the idea may be to our present society, education *is* a family function. No school can hope to serve in any greater capacity than as an extension of parental responsibility. Our present highly politicized compulsory educational system is a significant failure in that regard. The present publicly financed educational bureaucracy aggressively asserts its 'social' educational goals and denies the primary parental responsibility. The result has not only undercut the family function, but has set in motion a standardized, enmassed educational operation wonderfully adept at the making of mass-men."[3]

There is little on the Carter public record that reflects an understanding of this problem. His position on public education is generally the shallow response of most politicians: spend more public money.

His concern for the family structure has been made clear. In his first major speech after his nomination before a Manchester, New Hampshire, audience in August 1976 he made an unambiguous pledge concerning the family: "We are going to reverse the trend that we've experienced in the past that has destroyed the American family. . . . I believe we can restore what was lost," he added, without specifying what had weakened the family structure. "I believe we can bind our people back together. I believe we can restore human values, respect for one another, intimacy, love, respect for the law, patriotism, good education, strong churches, a good relationship among our people and government. I pledge to you that every statement I make, every decision I make, will give our families a decent chance to be strong again."[4] Just how a national government can achieve these goals was not made clear.

What makes this pledge suspect is the political alliance Carter had just concluded with the powerful liberal labor union, the National Education Association (NEA). NEA, along with other liberal educators, bears the major burden of responsibility for undermining the family and control of parents over their children.

From the start of his campaign for the nomination, Carter has courted NEA. "Carter has been wooing the NEA for almost two years," labor columnist Victor Riesel observed shortly before the Democratic Convention, "meeting with them regularly and at least five times since his Iowa [primary] victory."[5] At its June 1976 national convention, NEA hinted that its 1.8 million members might support Carter and its millions in political funds might be thrown behind Carter to ensure his election. Of the 600 union delegates at the Democratic National Convention, 170 were NEA members. NEA Executive Director Terry Herdon revealed that during the convention he met with Carter for thirty minutes and discussed the choice of a vice presidential running mate, favoring Sen. Walter Mondale and Sen. Edmund Muskie. NEA delegates initially planned independently to endorse Mondale, but later dropped the idea. Most likely, Carter's choice of Mondale had already been made, since the union bosses virtually controlled the convention and Carter.

Senator Mondale has long been a friend of NEA, and one of its most vocal supporters for spending taxpayers' billions for public education. Interestingly, Mondale's brother, Mort, is with the NEA affiliate, the South Dakota Educational Association.[6] Carter's wooing of this group, a group with power to siphon off billions from the American public purse, stands in sharp contrast to his former criticism of government by powerful elite groups. For NEA is a powerful elite that bears a substantial portion of responsibility for the decaying public education system. Nevertheless, Carter has promised to furnish still more billions in return for support at the polls. And NEA is pushing for even greater government social programs. "The National Education Association believes," states its Legislative Program, "that the two critical legislative issues to be pursued are the expansion and guaranteeing of the human and civil rights of all citizens and the *restructuring of national thinking in such a way as to emphasize finding cures for press-*

ing domestic problems and needs."[7] (Author's emphasis.)

Beyond spending additional billions allegedly for public education, NEA supports busing, sex education in the schools, abortion on demand, and a long list of social programs that not only have little to do with genuine education, but have contributed to undermining the American family and angered millions of parents. For example, busing and racial quotas, labeled as "affirmative action," have angered both blacks and whites. Yet Carter and the NEA continue to support this reverse form of racism. "We support continued adherence to the principle of affirmative action," stated Linda Chavez of NEA, "and urge that the higher education community, with the support of the federal government, develop and implement affirmative action programs suited to its needs."[8]

The anger of working-class Americans over the pursuit of this new racism in employment, enforced by the federal government, is equalled by the anger of many American academicians over sexual and racial quotas for higher institutions of learning. This is particularly true of the changes made in response to the violent assault on education by the New Left radicals in the last decade. "Clearly, beyond violence and its immediate consequences," observed Dr. L. G. Heller, Professor of Classical Languages and Hebrew at the City College of New York, "the American higher educational system faces many serious threats. The affirmative-action program, vigorously and stupidly pursued in the name of equality, threatens standards already eroded to a devastating degree."[9]

Carter's alliance with the NEA is with an organization that appears interested in spending billions for social engineering rather than for basic education. "A close examination of our numerous federal aid to education programs," notes Peter Witonski in a recent work on the crisis in education, "reveals a style of legislation that appears to be bent more on altering the social order of America than on improving our schools and universities."[10]

NEA continues to pursue such policies for "restructuring national thinking" while the fundamental purposes of education such as reading are ignored. "The very fact," writes Samuel Blumenfeld in his study of illiteracy, "that the federal government has to launch a Right-to-Read program is enough to indicate that there is something desperately wrong with the reading instruction which is being dispensed in our schools at the cost of billions each year. Never have so many children spent so much time in school, and never have we had so much functional illiteracy."[11]

Despite this state of affairs, organizations like NEA continue to pursue extraneous programs, such as public school sex education. This specific course of instruction is not only the most powerful instrument for undermining the American family in the crucial area of moral development; it is a major force for shaping values of young children about human sexual behavior that are a repudiation of the Judeo-Christian values that Jimmy Carter says he supports and wants to strengthen. "Public sex education," observes Gloria Lentz in her published work on the subject, "was begun in many areas on the premise that it would help curb social ills. But the reverse has happened. . . . Meanwhile, the sex educators, making a bundle of money, laugh all the way to the bank as we, the parents, permit them morally to bankrupt our children.

"The public school system," she adds, as it is represented today gives a parent no free choice to determine what is morally or religiously right for his child. His rights have been usurped by the bureaucracy of education.[12]

Viewed in its totality, the NEA program—which Carter has openly supported since he, by pledging more of the angry taxpayers' wages on it—views education as a tool for something more than education. Rather, it has a pronounced similarity to a program that repudiates the right of parents to control the destiny of their own children. This idea that the national government shall have complete control of a nation's children is remarkably similar to totalitarian regimes of the twentieth century. "There is a strong presumption among those who would use the state to bring about the good society," write Professor Benjamin A. Rogge and educator Pierre F. Goodrich, "to distrust the decision-making of the family in many areas, particularly in the rearing and education of the young. In almost all of the better-known Utopian schemes . . . the children are to be taken from their parents at an early age so that their upbringing can be under the control of the all-wise agents of the state, rather than of the foolish and primitive family circle."[13]

Jimmy Carter's political alliance with the NEA while pledging to strengthen the "American family structure" that "has been weakened" suggests a degree of ignorance—or opportunism—unprecedented in an American political candidate for President.

NOTES

1. Anne Husted Burleigh, Editor, *Education in a Free Society* (Indianapolis, Ind.: Liberty Fund, Inc., 1973) p. 3.
2. Jimmy Carter, *Why Not the Best?* p. 29.
3. George Charles Roche, III, *The Bewildered Society* (New Rochelle, N.Y.: Arlington House, 1972; paperback ed., Hillsdale Mich.: Hillsdale College Press, 1974) p. 313.
4. "Carter in New Hampshire, Promises to Seek to Restore Respect for Family," *The New York Times,* August 4, 1976.
5. "Carter Wooing Labor's COPE into Camp," *Baton Rouge* (La.) *Advocate*, June 22, 1976.
6. Education Daily, July 21, 1976, p. 3.
7. NEA Legislative Program 1975 (Washington, D.C.: National Education Association, July 1974.)
8. Statement, National Education Association Before the Office of Federal Contract Compliance, U.S. Dept. of Labor, August 22, 1976, p.1.
9. L. G. Heller, *The Death of the American University* (New Rochelle, N.Y.: Arlington House, 1973) p. 201.
10. Peter Witonski, *What Went Wrong with American Education And How to Make it Right* (New Rochelle, N.Y.: Arlington House, 1973) p. 122.

11. Samuel Blumenfeld, *The New Illiterates* (New Rochelle, N.Y.: Arlington House, 1973) p. 9.
12. Gloria Lentz, *Raping Our Children, The Sex Educational Scandal* (New Rochelle, N.Y.: Arlington House, 1972), pp. 216, 219.
13. Anne Husted Burleigh, Editor, *Education in a Free Society*, p. 37.

"New York's problems are a foretaste
of what other cities, states and the
country as a whole can expect. . . ."
—Milton Friedman
(November 17, 1975)

21

The Barefoot Boy and the Urban Bailout

Jimmy Carter, the southern barefoot boy from Plains, Georgia, may yet show himself to be the political savior of northern-urban liberalism.

Less than one year before Carter's nomination in the nation's largest urban center, New York City was confronted with its most far-reaching fiscal crisis of the century. While most Democrat liberals were reluctant to fix responsibility, Theodore H. White, the political chronicler of presidential elections, was more candid. In White's view, the New York City crisis was the direct result of "humanitarian" programs advocated by the Democratic Party and pursued to an extreme by the city. White was particularly harsh in his criticism of Lyndon B. Johnson who, he contends, pushed humanitarianism "by war abroad and by the Great Society at home, far beyond the limits of responsible government."[1]

Nevertheless, in his acceptance speech in New York City, Carter singled out Johnson for special praise. After praising Roosevelt, Truman and Kennedy, he said of LBJ: "And ours is also the party of a great-hearted Texan who took office in a tragic hour and who went on to do more than any other President in this century to advance the cause of human rights—Lyndon Johnson."[2]

Most of the national and New York local news media failed to analyze how and why the nation's largest and richest city, dominated by liberalism for decades, could present the spectacle of a pauper pleading for federal handouts. One exception was Ken Auletta of *New York* magazine. "We have conducted a noble experiment in local socialism and income redistribution," he wrote after an exhaustive examination of the crisis, "one clear result of which has been to redistribute much of our tax base and many jobs out of the city.

"The city's now overwhelming credit crisis is primarily a symptom, not a cause, of a deeper economic malaise, whose roots reach back three decades and encompass a series of city, state and even federal decisions. . . .

"If there is a single common thread weaving through these many decisions," he added, "it would be what is called 'politics.' And since 'liberal' politicians have dominated city government these many years it is they who are more guilty than others. The rollovers, false revenue estimates, and plain lies that have robbed taxpayers of literally billions through excessive borrowing to cover up excessive fraud . . . people have gone to jail for less."[3]

The four New York politicians regarded by Auletta as "the chief villains" are former Mayor Robert Wagner, former New York State Governor Nelson Rockefeller, former Mayor John Lindsay, and former City Comptroller Abraham Beame, currently Mayor in 1976. Auletta continues, "it must be remembered that they could not have accomplished all they did without a supporting cast of state legislators, borough presidents, City Council members and city comptrollers."[4]

This view was apparently not shared by Jimmy Carter who appeared proud when, on May 26, 1976, Mayor Beame endorsed him as "a friend" of New Yorkers. Beame claimed that Carter had "committed himself clearly and unhesitatingly to a body of programs and policies that will brighten the face of urban America and help bring hope and prosperity to our city and its people."[5] To make that statement, Beame had to ignore statements Carter had made as recently as two months earlier.

Carter continued to maintain that these program pledges were "consistent" with his previous statements and "he denied that he was changing his position" because of Mayor Beame's endorsement. But *The New York Times* remembered. "However, he had earlier declared that as President he would deal with the city only as part of an overall urban program rather than as a special program," the *Times* observed.[6]

In fact, on March 30, 1976, two months before Beame's endorsement and still facing primaries in states hostile to special favors for New York City, Carter told a group of *New York Times* reporters that it "would be inappropriate for the Federal government to single out New York City for special favors," and that he was against a complete national takeover of welfare from cities and states. "I think the Federal and the state governments," he said, "ought to share the responsibilities for welfare. The local government shouldn't have to pay any of it. But you would have an enormous additional cost shifted to the Federal Government if the system was completely Federalized with no commensurate increase in the quality of services to the people and as the welfare costs increase in future years it might be that the Federal Government could pick up the entire increase, but I would not want merely to shift the present welfare responsibility from the states entirely to the Federal Government."[7]

This is Carter at his shiftiest. This sort of statement gives him room to go in either direction. In his meeting with Mayor Beame in May, for example, it was not clear whether pledges to Beame by Carter meant just New York City. The mayor's press secretary Sid Frigand said at the time of the endorsement that Carter, in a series of discussions ranging over several weeks prior to Beame's endorsement, had emerged with a "sharpened position" on special federal favors for the city and a takeover by Washington on the city welfare system.[8] But no doubt existed that by the time the Carter Party Platform was written both he and the Democratic Party were in favor of a Federal welfare takeover, replacing welfare with a guaranteed annual income "substantially financed by the Federal government" while acknowledging that this reform may require an additional investment. . . .

"As an interim step," the plank adds, "and as a means of providing immediate federal fiscal relief to state and local governments, local governments should no longer be required to bear the burden of welfare costs. Further, *there should be a phased reduction in the state's share of welfare costs*."[9] (Author's emphasis.)

This Carterizing of the truth on issues was a fairly common technique. In November 1975, for example, Carter raised serious questions and doubts that the Ford Administration's federal loans to New York City might set a dangerous precedent for other cities. At that time, polls indicated considerable national hostility to the Ford administration's bail-out plan for the city. And, too, Carter was then facing primaries in more conservative states like New Hampshire, Florida and North Carolina. But he had won in those states by late March, and he quietly shifted toward bail-out for New York City; suggestions of a Federal takeover of welfare at the local level helped him in Ohio, New Jersey and California. It was only *after* the June 8 primaries that Carter fully revealed the extent of his plans to bail out northern urban cities and states. In his speech before the U.S. Conference of Mayors in Milwaukee, Carter went all the way, calling for national programs like those created by Franklin Roosevelt and the New Deal in the 1930s.[10] Without being specific or providing a price tag, Carter proposed that national money be earmarked for specific urban problems, offering federal aid for low-cost public housing, funds for urban transit and anti-recession measures, such as federal government work programs like the New Deal's Works Project Administration (WPA).[11]

His Milwaukee proposals were far removed from his conservative anti-Washington and anti-bureaucracy campaign in the primaries that had won him moderate and conservative votes. Apparently his campaign to gain backing of big-city Democratic leaders and liberals began in earnest weeks before Mayor Beame's endorsement and continued right up to the convention when he chose Mondale as his running mate. The wholescale scuttling of his primary campaign pledges to shake up the Washington bureaucracy—while obviously planning once in power to expand that bureaucracy—could be justified by his supporters on the grounds that he had to promise to bail out the urban liberal big cities if he was not only to secure the nomination but win the election.

Significantly, in the same week that Carter gained Beame's endorsement the liberal Brookings Institution of Washington, D.C., conveniently released a study that Carter could use to rationalize the abandonment of his former anti-bureaucracy crusade. In short, what the Brookings study said was that efforts to stop the rapid growth of government agencies were impossible.[12] It appears to be no accident that the study was released at a time when Carter was moving to dump his anti-bureaucracy stance and shift to the left to gain the support of urban liberals with promises of more national programs, particularly since Brookings has closely advised the Carter campaign from the very beginning.

Carter's courting of northern urban liberals had both immediate and long-range implications. Immediately, it offered the Beame administration the opportunity to default on the promises made to the Ford administration in late 1975 when the national government approved federally guaranteed loans. The Beame administration indicated that it would delay fiscal reforms demanded by the Ford administration, believing that Carter's victory would bring to power an administration willing to be more lenient with the city. Carter's urban bail-out program held out the promise of saving the political fortunes of New York and other cities threatened with certain political defeat because of growing taxes, huge welfare rolls and general urban decay. In agreeing to shift the burden of welfare schemes and social programs from the northern urban cities the states to the national level, Carter had assured himself of the nomination and strong backing of the northern big cities in the presidential campaign.

Still, he had proposed no specific way to come to grips with the crisis that had brought New York City to the brink of fiscal insolvency. Rather, his program—the platform of his party—appears to be a prescription for duplicating the New York disaster at the national level. The very proposals that wrecked New York City have been reiterated in the 1976 Democratic Platform and are now offered to the nation as "new ideas and new leadership"; proposals such as government planning, subsidy, controls on business and individuals, and other social-engineering schemes that destroyed more in New York City than they built.

Jane Jacobs, in her classic work *The Death and Life of American Cities,* published in 1961, identified the myth of liberal northern urban planners that large amounts of public money could cure city problems. "This is not the rebuilding of cities," she wrote. "This is the sacking of cities."[13]

Jacobs provided an illustration of government urban renewal programs launched in the late 1940s, and their effect of New York's East Harlem. "The more that poured in," she noted of government money, "the worse became the turmoils and troubles of East Harlem, and still more did it become like a deprived, backward country. More than 1,300 businesses which had the misfortune to occupy sites marked for housing were wiped away, and an estimated four-fifths of the proprietors ruined. . . . Virtually all the unslummed population which had hung on was rooted out and dispersed to 'better itself.' "[14]

In the fourteen years since these words were written, billions of local, state, and Federal aid dollars have been poured into northern urban areas. Ironically, the results were reported in *The New York Times* two days before the adoption of the Democratic Platform. "The older neighborhoods in the center of large industrial cities," reported *The Times,* "despite the infusion of Federal and private antipoverty money in the 1960's, emerged from the decade in some respects worse off than they began it, according to a study by the National Center for Urban Affairs [Washington, D.C.]."[15]

Jimmy Carter the southerner is leading a band of northern urban liberals and union bosses on a political march to duplicate nationwide what had been done to New York City and other large northern urban areas. "New York's lavish spending," warned economist Milton Friedman, "reflects the most welfare-state-oriented electorate in the U.S. In this sense, New York's problems are a foretaste of what other cities, other states and the country as a whole can expect if their electorate continue to imitate New York's left surge. Trying to do good by spending someone else's money is a sure-fire recipe for financial disaster. If New York City does not persuade you of that, simply cast your eyes across the Atlantic to Great Britain."[16]

NOTES

1. "Liberalism Unmasked," *Richmond Times Dispatch* editorial, (based on an article in *New York* magazine) November 10, 1975.
2. Carter's Acceptance Speech, text reprinted in *U.S. News and World Report,* July 26, 1976.
3. "Who's to Blame for the Fix We're In," *New York,* October 27, 1975.
4. "Who's to Blame for the Fix We're In."
5. "Carter Pledges Aid for City, Wins Beame Backing," *The New York Times,* May 27, 1976.
6. "Carter Pledges Aid for City, Wins Beame Backing."
7. *The New York Times* interview with Jimmy Carter on urban affairs, March 31, 1976.
8. "Why Beame Backs Carter," *New York Post,* May 27, 1976.
9. The National Democratic Platform 1976, *Welfare Reform,"* p. 21.

10. "Carter Gives Cities Priority," *The Raleigh (N.C.) Times*, June 30, 1976.
11. "Urban Stand Outlined by Carter," *Richmond Times Dispatch* June 30, 1976.
12. "Cut in Bureaucracy Called Unlikely." *Richmond Times Dispatch*, May 28, 1976.
13. Jane Jacobs, *The Death and Life of American Cities* (New York: Vintage Books—Random House, 1961), p. 4.
14. Jane Jacobs, *The Death and Life of American Cities.*
15. "Poverty Found to Persist in Older Inner Cities Despite Aid Plans," *The New York Times*, July 12, 1976.
16. "New York City," *Newsweek*, November 17, 1975.

"The ultimate goal is total disarmament, internally and internationally. . . ."
—Richard C. Clark
The Road to Revolution

22

Disarmament: The Grand Delusion

The idea of disarmament—whether outlawing private ownership of firearms at home or banning of nuclear weapons and conventional arms by agreement abroad—flows from a grand delusion: that violence and war can be contained and controlled if weapons are outlawed. The consistent failure of domestic gun control laws and of international disarmament agreements over the decades do not deter the advocates of this dual delusion.

Jimmy Carter favors both domestic and international disarmament.* In doing so he undercuts the most fundamental right of an individual and of a nation: *the right of self-defense*. This is strange for a southerner and former U.S. Navy officer. Historically, the South has always been the strongest advocate of self-defense, both personal and in the maintenance of strong national defense posture. This attitude is reflected in the high percentage of southerners who enter the American military and the fact that the ownership of firearms is the highest in the South.[1]

Despite the belief that the ownership of firearms is growing the fastest in northern crime-ridden urban cen-

* For a more detailed analysis of Carter's position on domestic gun controls see Jeffrey St. John, "The Right to Keep and Bear Arms," in *Guns and Ammo,* October 1976 (8490 Sunset Blvd., Los Angeles, Ca. 90069).

ters, "gun owners are more often middle-class folk from small or rural communities in the South."[2] Thus the Carter proposal for controlling firearms in the name of combatting crime would most directly affect his native South.

The Democratic Platform, to which Carter is pledged, maintains that while the Democrats support "the right of sportsmen to possess guns for purely hunting and target-shooting purposes," they want a national-state program to control handguns. "Handguns simplify and intensify violent crime," states the gun control plank in the Platform. "Ways must be found to curtail the availability of these weapons. The Democratic Party must provide the leadership for a coordinated federal and state effort to strengthen the presently inadequate controls over the manufacture, assembly, distribution, and possession of handguns and to ban Saturday night specials."[3]

Several states now have strong laws designed to curb the possession and use of firearms. Do the existing state laws controlling guns work?

In the same month the above plank was drafted (June 1976) a significant finding was reported in a national magazine. The report, in *Human Behavior*, stated, "The University of Wisconsin's Douglas R. Murray says no, after surveying the gun control policies of all 50 states and comparing them with each state's crime statistics. Not only do restrictions fail to inhibit violence, but not one of the seven laws he considered (license to purchase, waiting period before delivery, police record of sales, license to sell retail, minimum age, permit to carry openly and permit to carry concealed) had any significant effect on homicide, assault, robbery, suicide or accidents."[4]

During the writing of the Platform plank on gun control the Carter forces apparently sought to minimize the implications of their proposals. At least this was the assessment of the only member of the Platform Committee to vote against the gun-control plank in particular, and the entire Platform in general. "They (Carter's people) tried to keep everything under cover," stated Louisiana State Representative Louis "Woody" Jenkins. "The banning of handguns, for example, was kept vague and we do not know whether this would be a first step toward the party's long-standing commitment to the licensing and registration of all gun owners. There is no sentiment in the platform that every American has a constitutional right to 'Keep and Bear Arms!' "[5]

Jenkins' suspicions are supported by additional evidence. Since Franklin Roosevelt, the Democratic Party has been the most persistent advocate of domestic disarmament. During the Johnson administration, and in the wake of the assassinations of Dr. Martin Luther King Jr., and Senator Robert F. Kennedy in 1968, the strongest anti-gun legislation was passed. Leading that campaign was Johnson's presidential assistant Joseph Califano.[6] Califano was appointed by Carter as a domestic advisor.[7] Carter's running mate, Senator Walter Mondale, has also been a strong advocate of gun control.

Carter's principal fund raiser, Maurice Dees, is the architect of an anti-gun lobby group called the National Gun Control Center (NGCC). John Heath, a Washington spokesman for NGCC, said shortly before the Democratic Convention that the "eventual aim of the Center is a complete ban on handguns" and he refused to rule out a ban on rifles. "The details will have to be worked out," he said.[8]

Earlier, however, the founder of NGCC, Maurice Dees, had been very specific about the goals of the organization. "Within five years," he stated, "we will break the National Rifle Association."[9]

Dees serves as Vice Chairperson of the NGCC; Carter supporter Atlanta Mayor Maynard Jackson is Chairperson and other well-known Carter supporters and advisors on the National Committee are Congressman Andrew Young (Georgia) and Ted Sorenson, formerly a speechwriter for John F. Kennedy. "The National Gun Control Center," wrote Jackson in a fund-raising letter sent out in the Spring of 1976, "is seeking one million members to fund a national educational program to tell the other side of the story."[10]

As president, Carter would be in a powerful position to enact a far-reaching domestic disarmament program. Various key Democratic leaders in the House and Senate could push through such a program while the National Gun Control Center could orchestrate an "educational program" in the national media, which is already committed to extensive controls on private ownership of all firearms.

Professor Richard C. Clark, associate professor of government and politics at St. John's University, New York City, identifies the paradox of favoring domestic disarmament in the face of rising crime and the mushrooming of domestic terrorist groups. While the media clamors for the abrogation of the Second Amendment (the right to bear arms) it evades the insidious misuse of the First Amendment (freedom of speech and expression) by domestic terrorist groups who freely circulate literature to support their terrorist activities. "Throughout history," Clark writes, "few arguments have been more seductively hypocritical than those of the elitist organs of the media on 'gun control.' In misleading the public on the causes of violence in this nation, they are either hopelessly naive or viciously sinister. No other conclusion can be prudently drawn. Hunter, sportsmen, target shooters, etc., are under constant attack and blame, but violent terrorists enjoy sanctuaries for their openly and clearly professed program to destroy the nation's institutions."[11]

The Democratic Platform contains no plank that specifically condemns *domestic* terrorism of the sort that has mushroomed in the United States in recent years. It does, however, have a plank that condemns *international* terrorism. This inclusion results from pressure from pro-Israeli delegates, especially after the dramatic Israeli raid to rescue hostages held in Uganda by pro-Palestinian terrorist hijackers.

This condition of selective blindness carries over to the area of international disarmament as well. The platform writers evade the fact that crime and violence are caused by criminals, and then seek to control crime by disarming the innocent citizens; in the same way they attempt to subdue international violence by disarming the nonaggressive nations. Armed robbers will not respond to gun control laws by throwing down their guns, nor will detente or any other restrictive agreement deter militaristic nations from making wars. International disarmament is viewed by the Soviet Union as a vital part of its program of deception to weaken the West, particularly the United States. In calling for "nuclear disarmament and arms control" agreements with the Soviet Union, Carter and the Democratic Party are committing the same evasions as they are in advocating a domestic program of control of firearms.

In the face of all the evidence then—historical, logical, demonstrable facts—that state laws against guns do not disarm criminals and international peace treaties do not disarm militaristic nations, how can the supporters of these measures continue to advocate them? Professor Clark attributes this view to a combination of delusion and deception. The delusion is self-induced; the deception is practiced by those who have an interest in disarming the victims. "But the ultimate goal," he concludes, "is total disarmament, internally and internationally, as America's contribution to 'perpetual peace.' "[12]

NOTES

1. George D. Newton and Franklin E. Zimring, *Firearms and Violence in American Life*, a staff report to the National Commission on the Causes and Prevention of Violence (Washington, D.C., U.S. Government Printing Office, 1970), p. 10.
2. "A Loaded Issue," *Human Behavior*, June, 1976.
3. The National Democratic Platform 1976, "Law Enforcement and Law Observance," p. 35.
4. "A Loaded Issue."
5. "Jenkins Critical of Demo Platform," *Baton Rouge Advocate*, June 19, 1976.
6. "A Question of Guns," *Newsweek*, June 24, 1976.
7. "The Carter Brain Trust," *Newsweek*, June 21, 1976.

8. "New Anti-Gun Group Has Roots in Jimmy Carter's Entourage," *National Catholic Register*, June 27, 1976.
9. Quoted in Garry Wills' column, *Rocky Mountain News* (Denver), April 8, 1976.
10. Fund-raising letter, the National Gun Control Center, 1201 Connecticut Avenue, N.W., Washington, D.C. 20036, April 23, 1976.
11. "Hypocrisy on 'Gun Control,'" *State of the Nation* (newsletter), Vol. 8, No. 3, March 1976. Adapted from a chapter in Richard C. Clark, *The Road to Revolution* (Old Greenwich, Conn.: Devin-Adair, forthcoming.)
12. "Hypocrisy on 'Gun Control.'"

"Friends of his in Georgia are worried about his stubbornness. . . . Woodrow Wilson was also a very stubborn man."

—Henry Brandon, Journalist
Sunday Times of London
(August 1976)

23

Welfare Worker to the World

No part of the Jimmy Carter program suffers more from inherent personal and policy weakness than his world outlook and the way he proposes to use American power in foreign affairs. His world view is drawn from the disasters of the past.

With one exception Carter has surrounded himself with foreign policy advisors who have been influential in the two previous Democratic administrations. John F. Kennedy and Lyndon B. Johnson were the architects of American foreign policy disasters in the 1960s—Bay of Pigs, Berlin Wall, Cuban Missile Crisis, the Communist takeovers in Vietnam, Cambodia, and Laos. Ignoring this glaring truth in the presidential campaign, Carter glibly explained away the Southeast Asian disaster as occurring because the United States "did things that were contrary to our basic character. The lesson we draw from recent history," Carter states, "is that public understanding and support are now as vital to a successful foreign policy as they are to any domestic program."[1]

Public support for the Vietnam war began to disintegrate under the Johnson Administration's piecemeal policy approach and the impact of anti-war propaganda. The opportunism of liberal-to-left members of Mr. Carter's own party also played a role. Carter himself displayed a talent for changing sides when it proved politically expedient. "Mr. Carter's support of the war," wrote Charles Mohr of *The New York Times,* "was one of the most prolonged and persistent of any major political figure. He attempted to dissuade fellow governors from condemning American involvement in the conflict and told journalists as late as 1974 that he favored continued Administration requests for more appropriation for the war."[2]

But as a presidential candidate, Carter condemned the Vietnam war as "racist" and proposed that one of his first acts as President would be to issue a blanket pardon for draft dodgers. (He was roundly booed for this statement at the national convention of the American Legion in Seattle on August 24, 1976.)

An angry columnist went into print looking for answers to these paradoxes. "Since you, sir, were among the foremost supporters of the war effort," wrote Patrick J. Buchanan, "when did you discover it was racist? Was it after studying reports of the attitude of U.S. field commanders? Was it after consulting the theologians? Or was it perhaps when you found out that the surest way to win over the anti-Carter liberals in the Democratic party is to vomit on the U.S. military effort in Vietnam?

"One wonders why this man of God, this 'born again' Christian, should be struggling with such purpose and tenacity to become commander-in-chief of the selfsame armed forces who waged that 'racist' war in Southeast Asia."[3]

In another policy reversal Carter, at a Las Vegas press conference in May 1976 denied that he ever supported Army First Lt. William L. Calley, Jr., convicted by an Army Court Martial of murdering 22 Vietnamese civilians.[4] But in 1971 it was a different story. "Georgia's Gov. Jimmy Carter," *Newsweek* noted, describing the angry reaction after the April 1971 conviction of Calley, "proclaimed an 'American Fighting Man's Day' this week and asked citizens to drive with their auto headlights turned on."[5]

Carter's talent for twisting the truth to suit his audience and his willingness to appease the extreme left elements of his party indicate that in foreign policy he might be the prisoner of domestic political pressure groups. His alliance with blacks, for example, has virtually dictated a hostility toward white-ruled South Africa and Rhodesia, while his willingness to pursue agreements with the Soviets to reduce tensions are not much different from the policies pursued by John F. Kennedy, Lyndon B. Johnson, Richard Nixon, and Gerald Ford.

Perhaps what finally distinguishes him from past presidents in foreign policy are the ambitious goals he supports in the face of a lack of any real solid experience. "If Jimmy Carter is elected President in November," wrote William V. Shannon of *The New York Times* shortly before the Democratic convention, "the early signs point toward his trying to act out the same impossible dream that John F. Kennedy attempted when he organized the foreign affairs side of his Administration in 1960. Like Kennedy, Mr. Carter is keenly interested in foreign affairs without ever having any experience, aside from reading and travel, in the actual conduct of diplomacy. Notwithstanding his inexperience, he, too, is determined to keep the decision-making powers in his own hands."

Shannon added: "A President who cares very little about domestic problems can afford to devote long hours to managing his foreign policy. But Mr. Carter who intends to reorganize the entire Federal Government and put through an ambitious program will find the domestic political management of his foreign policy problems a severe distraction."[6]

Carter's well-known stubbornness and volatile temperament, so successfully hidden beneath a publicly smiling exterior, could serve to compound his problems, particularly if a combination of a Republican opposition, a critical press and an unwilling Congress sought to oppose him on his domestic reorganization and his foreign policy goals. ". . . certain aspects of his character make one a little hesitant," stated Henry Brandon, a British journalist based in Washington. "I don't regard him as devious. I just regard him as a natural politician. . . .

"Some friends of his in Georgia," Brandon adds, "are worried about his stubbornness and where this is going to lead him if he becomes President. Woodrow Wilson was also a very stubborn man and his stubbornness led to such a stalemate with Congress that he failed to achieve what he most wanted. This could happen to Carter, judging by the way he handled the state legislature in Georgia."[7]

While many observers have compared Carter with Richard M. Nixon, citing the similarity of their solitary aloofness and cold, withdrawn relationship even with closest associates, Carter perhaps most resembles Woodrow Wilson, the president that Nixon always said *he* most admired. The similarity extends to Carter's moralizing sermonettes, for which Wilson was famous. "It must be the responsibility of the President to restore the moral authority of this country in its conduct of foreign policy," Carter told the liberal Council on Foreign Relations in Chicago. "We should work for peace and the control of arms in everything we do. We should support the humanitarian aspirations of the world's people. Policies that strengthen dictators or create refugees, policies that prolong suffering or postpone racial justice weaken that authority. Policies that encourage economic progress and social justice promote it."[8]

This high moral tone is challenged by his record of expediency on the Vietnam war, and suggests that Carter would be different from past presidents in the conduct of foreign policy in that he would be less willing to face the realities of totalitarian aggressive Communist power and would be more willing to become a Wilsonian welfare worker of the world. In short, Carter would be an international flower child in his conduct of foreign policy. This possibility is clearly foretold in the party platform, written and adopted largely by a party and a convention dominated by the political shapers of the 1960s. Greater stress is given to agreements and worldwide welfare projects than to traditional U.S. defense commitments and treaties, although the Carter platform pays lip service to the military alliances of the United States and, not surprisingly, stresses a need for a strong navy.

Carter's foreign policy proposals, like those of Woodrow Wilson, made broad assumptions rooted more in theory than in reality. For example, the plank on Asia: "We reaffirm our commitment to the security of the Republic of Korea, both in itself and as a key to the security of Japan. However, on a prudent and carefully planned basis, we can redeploy, and gradually phase out, the U.S. ground forces, and can withdraw the nuclear weapons now stationed in Korea without endangering that support, as long as our tactical air and naval forces in the region remain strong."[9]

On August 18, only five weeks after the above plank was approved, North Koreans brutally murdered two American army officers in the demilitarized zone.[10] For months prior to the incident Carter's political allies had been condemning South Korea for its alleged brutal and repressive regime. Overseas, at an 85-nation conference, the socialist nonaligned third-world nations used these recent atrocities as one more opportunity to demand that the United States leave Korea *and* give up control of the Panama Canal.[11] Despite this long-standing hostility against the United States there is a call in the platform to aid the third-world nations.

Carter's policy toward Communist Cuba is another illustration of how his theory clashes with reality. The Platform calls for "relations with Cuba" *if* Cuba refrains from "interference in the internal affairs of other nations." The same document asks for normalization of relations with Communist Angola, which Cuba helped conquer. This indirect sanction of Cuban aggression is even more questionable in view of the growing body of evidence to show not only that Castro is continuing to engage in subversive activities against the United States, but may actually have been directly involved in the assassination of John F. Kennedy. Evidence produced by a Senate investigation in

1975-76 points directly to Castro. As recently as August 22, 1976, new evidence was presented. "Long before his recent murder," reported the Washington *Post,* "John Rosselli, the CIA's underworld recruit in attempts to kill Fidel Castro, had been privately claiming that agents of the Cuban premier, in retaliation, were involved in the assassination of President John F. Kennedy."[12]

The era of JFK began with idealism similar to Woodrow Wilson's. Carter's outlook most resembles Wilson in this regard, rather than Roosevelt, Truman, Kennedy or Johnson. As an engineer with an engineer's education, instead of a southern education with respect for classical culture and roots, Carter only thinks of human problems to be structured and forced, if necessary, into rigid forms. His views of foreign policy, as reflected in the Platform, demonstrate this passion for engineering and a belief that peace, poverty and global conflict can be engineered into solutions. But problems, domestic or foreign, involve human beings, not rigid materials like cinder blocks and steel girders.

Woodrow Wilson, who had greater cultural and intellectual depth than Carter does, suffered from this same impersonalization of the human condition. Like Carter, he had very little real-life experience with a broad range of people. Wilson spent much of his time in the closed society of the university; Carter has spent much of his life in the closed societies of the Navy and of Plains, Georgia. Wilson set out to make a permanent peace after World War I and, instead, set the stage for a second war in Europe and began the lethal process of expanding the powers of the American presidency.

"Wilson saw himself," observed the historian James David Barber, "as one of those [who knew how to see the good and make it happen], a man destined to make the world's salvation part of his own. He joined to this religiously based world view an almost mystical faith in the democratic spirit. 'The people' to Wilson were the bearers of an innate rightness, masked at times by the confusions of the world, but capable, when rightly informed and inspired, of pointing out the path. . . . Wilson *knew*, as surely as he knew God's will, that the people were with him."[13]

NOTES

1. Jimmy Carter, speech to the Council on Foreign Relations, Chicago. Reprinted in *Congressional Record*, May 11, 1976, p. 6823.
2. "Carter Credibility Issue: Calley and Vietnam War," *The New York Times*, May 21, 1976.
3. "Carter's Comment on the 'Racist War," *Richmond Times-Dispatch*, May 26, 1976.
4. "Carter Credibility Issue."
5. "Judgment at Fort Benning," *Newsweek*, April 12, 1971. See also *National Observer*, April 5, 1971 and *Atlanta Constitution*, April 2, 1971.
6. "Remembering Mr. Rusk," *The New York Times*, July 8, 1976.
7. "A Hard Look at the Presidential Race: Keen Foreign Observers Assess the Campaign and Candidates," *Atlas*, August 1976.
8. Speech to the Council on Foreign Relations.
9. The National Democratic Platform 1976, "Asia," p. 66.
10. "North Koreans Kill Two American Officers," *Richmond Times-Dispatch*, August 19, 1976.
11. "3rd World Warns U.S. on Korea, Panama," *Richmond Times-Dispatch*, August 22, 1976.
12. "Slain Mobster Claimed Cuban Link to JFK Death," *Washington Post*, August 22, 1976.
13. James David Barber, *The Presidential Character: Predicting Performance in the White House* (Englewood Cliffs, N.J.: Prentice Hall, 1972.), p. 63.

"What they have wanted is a priest, not a politician."

—Bill Moyers,
CBS-TV
(July 15, 1976)

24

The Closed Convention

By the time the Democratic Convention rolled around, Jimmy Carter, the political and moral engineer, had put all the pieces together. As with the building of the ancient pyramids, he has built the structure of his political victory block by block. Even at the moment of his triumph, he surveyed the sea of cheering delegates at New York's Madison Square Garden with the outward coolness of a prince patiently waiting to be crowned king. "I am not easily overwhelmed," he later confessed, "and it was something that we had anticipated, obviously not a surprise. But I was surprised at the intensity of my feeling when I walked into the hall . . . the number of people there and the tightness of it, the sense of friendship toward me, the acceptability, the harmony."[1]

It was an admission that revealed a man permanently out of touch with an understanding of his own emotions and the realities of how and why he was able to pyramid a meager political career and experience into a triumph—towards which an average person might display an outward flush of emotion and exhilaration. "The camera caught him leaning hungrily and impatiently," reported *New York Times* TV critic John J. O'Connor, "toward three television cameras as New York prepared to announce its tally.

"Noticing that he was on the air, Mr. Carter recovered quickly and grabbed his infant grandson, providing a suitably 'warm' image for the national audience. For added impact, he later posed with his arm around his mother, the delightful Miss Lillian. Depending on vantage point, the new candidate might be considered either distressingly calculating or brilliantly composed."[2]

Like the monarch who believes that his subjects really love him and wish him to rule by reason of superior wisdom, Jimmy Carter indulged in the delusion that the majority of the delegates to the Democratic National Convention looked on him with love and friendship instead of as a means to power. The lure was being with the new "insider," not love or even harmony, or his highly vacillating and imprecise positions on issues. For a majority of the delegates polled by the *Washington Post* during the convention could not honestly say they knew just where Carter stood. "Along with the great numbers of other delegates to the Democratic National Convention," reported the *Post*, "these delegates are highly uncertain about the stand Jimmy Carter takes on many issues. They also share another conviction common at this convention. They believe that Carter will win in November."[3]

Of course, like his posing for the TV cameras during the convention after being caught off guard, the drive for the nomination had always been calculated by Carter on vague themes. How else could he manage to smuggle his socialist program into Washington? He couldn't repeat the strategic blunder of George McGovern of 1972 and openly tell the American people what plans he proposes. The delegates cynically understood the Carterizing of the truth by running against Washington and big government, while privately planning to make the national government bigger if not necessarily better. "This is reputed to be an anti-Washington year in politics," observed the *Washington Post*, "and Jimmy Carter is regarded as somehow an anti-Washington candidate. But don't let them fool you: The Democrats have not abandoned their traditional belief in big government.

"A majority of the delegates . . . would rather continue to have 'large government with many services' than go to 'smaller government with fewer services.' a survey by the *Washington Post* has found."[4]

New York Mayor Abraham Beame understood this better than the delegates. His assurances from Carter that his own political fortune and that of the city would be saved by dollars from taxpayers all over the country rightly gave him reason to paraphrase Mark Twain in his welcoming speech to the delegates that "reports of the death of this city had been exaggerated."[5] Later Beame would confess why the Democratic Party had worked so hard in 1975 to capture the convention for New York when the city seemed prepared to sink into a sea of red ink. "The tremendous exposure this event got in the news media in this country and abroad," said Jorgen Hansen, a close ally of Beame, "was great publicity for New York. It will surely offset the bad impression of the city that has been created in the past few years."[6]

Tom Bradley, black mayor of Los Angeles and co-chairman of the convention, is a politician who understood why harmony must be maintained even at the cost of suppressing views held by a majority of Americans on busing, abortion, gun control, runaway bureaucracy and deficit spending. "We are all Americans," he told the convention, "we come from neither North nor South, East nor West. What we need now is a Marshall Plan for the cities."[7] The Marshall Plan, a U.S.-sponsored European Recovery Program between 1948 and 1952 to restore war-ravaged Europe, cost American taxpayers $12 billion.[8] It was also the forerunner of the American foreign aid program that has spent, from the end of World War II to the present, in excess of $150 billion.[9]

In short, there was unity and harmony at the convention that nominated Jimmy Carter not out of principle but out of a hunger for pure power over the national government purse. Such control is already exercised by the Democrats' domination of the legislative branch. National Chairman Robert Strauss admitted this when he said, "between 1948 and 1976 we have been the majority party."[10]

David Broder of the *Washington Post* provided the most powerful metaphor in print. "A national convention," he wrote, "is a snapshot, taken at a single instant, of a political party whose institutional life spans the generations. It is a family reunion on a massive scale."[11]

Closer examination of a freeze frame of the Democratic family at its reunion in New York reveals conservatives of the party lulled by Carter's promises while fearful that too close a look might uncover the truth. Clearwater, Florida, lawyer Norman Bie, who confirmed for this writer that Carter forces rigged the straw poll at the Florida State convention in November 1975 (cited in the first chapter of this book), was typical of the conservative Wallace delegate. "I feel just fine about Carter," he said, "and I think he will be a good President. He isn't a socialist like Hubert Humphrey."

Nor does he perceive him to be a George McGovern, for he added, "McGovern and his bunch were bloodthirsty; they were going to carve a brave new world and do it with a bayonet."[12]

Black mayor of Gary, Indiana, Richard Hatcher expressed the consensus and confidence of the socialist wing of the party. "We always knew," Hatcher said, "what kind of person Jimmy Carter was by the Vice President he would choose. I am delighted he selected Walter Mondale."[13]

Mondale, the heir-apparent to the "socialist" Hubert Humphrey, summarized the expectations of all the delegates unified over the prospect of a plunder on the public treasury. "The first thing we are going to do," he said in his acceptance speech, "when Carter is elected, we are going to get this government moving again.

"We are a new generation of leadership," Mondale added, evading the history of his party since Franklin Roosevelt, "and we are strong and we are ready. The other party is pledged to the proposition that government doesn't work. We are pledged to make it work."[14]

CBS-TV commentator Eric Sevareid summed up Carter's acceptance speech best when he said, "What he is saying is that we can only be great through goodness. But this is a long laundry list that he laid out in his speech to help the poor."[15]

Sevareid's colleague, Bill Moyers, summed it all up when he said with wonder: "I have never seen such a combination of religion, politics, and manipulative techniques . . . what they [the delegates] have wanted is a priest, not a politician."[16]

NOTES

1. "He says Nomination Rite Was 'Highly Emotional,'" *The New York Times*, July 17, 1976.
2. "TV: The Convention Covers Itself," *The New York Times*, July 15, 1976.
3. "Uncertainty on Carter's Views," *Washington Post*, July 14, 1976.
4. "Survey: Democrats Still Favor Big Government," *Washington Post*, July 13, 1976.
5. Mayor Abraham Beame, text of speech, Madison Square Garden, New York City, July 12, 1976.
6. "Convention Is Described As Bringing a Legacy of Good Will to New York," *The New York Times*, July 18, 1976.
7. NBC-TV Convention coverage, July 13, 1976. 8:00 pm EDT.
8. *Micropaedia*, Vol. VI, p. 648.
9. "Foreign Aid: End of an Era?" *U.S. News & World Report*, November 15, 1971.
10. CBS-TV Convention coverage, July 12, 1976, 10:01 pm EDT.
11. "Intriguing Were the Glimpses of the Candidates-in-Waiting," *Richmond Times-Dispatch*, July 20, 1976.
12. "Why Nominate Carter" Disparate Delegates Declare, 'He Can Win,'" *Wall Street Journal*, July 13, 1976.
13. Interview, NBC-TV Convention coverage, July 15, 1976, 4:55 pm EDT.
14. ABC-TV Convention coverage, July 15, 1976, 10:07 pm EDT.

15. CBS-TV Convention coverage, July 15, 1976, 11:54 pm EDT.
16. CBS-TV Convention coverage, July 15, 1976, 11:54 pm EDT.

"Every time I hear a politician talk
about morality, my stomach tells
me he's out to get me."

—Michael Novak
Theologian-Philosopher
(April 1976)

25

The Theology of Power, The Priesthood of Politics

Has Jimmy Carter cynically exploited his religious "born-again" Christianity in the 1976 presidential campaign, as he has exploited and manipulated other issues?

Major questions were raised about his Southern Baptist religion and at the same time it evoked the memory of John F. Kennedy and the Catholic issue in the 1960 campaign—a campaign and style that Jimmy Carter studied closely and carefully. "There is a hidden religious power base in American culture," observed the Catholic theologian and writer Michael Novak, "which our secular biases prevent many of us from noticing. Jimmy Carter has found it. . . .

"Carter's role for evangelical Christians may be rather like John F. Kennedy's for Catholics . . ." Novak added, "in his voice they heard their own accent, and in their hearts they saw themselves as they would like to be."[1]

Novak points out that the most "underrated demographic reality in the United States is the huge number of evangelical Protestants, Jimmy Carter's natural constituency. They are to be found not only in the 'Bible Belt,' south of the Mason-Dixon Line, but all over the United States, in small towns and large cities. The lowest estimate of their numbers is 31 million; a plausible figure is 40 million—two-thirds of all white Protestants. Not all are Democrats; many outside the South are Republicans."[2]

Apparently Jimmy Carter calculated during the primaries that he needed to make a strong bid for this huge block. He did so with a boldness that offended the many northern liberals, especially Jews. After his nomination, and the capture of liberal, labor and urban northern blocs, his reference to his "born-again" Christian faith virtually disappeared, for it had been the subject of searching questions. His manipulation of the religious issue was revealed by Robert Shrum, a 32-year-old speechwriter for George McGovern who briefly served Carter before quitting and denouncing the candidate for being "deceptive and manipulative." According to Shrum, Carter ordered no more statements on the Middle East during his primary battles with Senator Henry Jackson (Democrat, Washington). "Jackson has all the Jews anyway," Shrum reported Carter saying, "I don't get over four percent of the Jewish vote anyway, so forget it. *We get the Christians.*"[3] (Author's emphasis.)

The suspicion that Carter has exploited his religion for political purposes is strengthened by the fact that very early Carter retained former speechwriter for John F. Kennedy, Theodore C. Sorensen. In 1956, when backing Kenndey for the vice presidency, Sorensen argued that far from hurting the presidential bid of Adlai Stevenson, JFK's Catholicism would help him. During the 1960 race, and since then, critics have charged that the Kennedy campaign exploited the Catholic issue so as to produce a "backlash against bigotry" and produce a sympathy vote for Kennedy against Richard Nixon. Sorensen has always been sensitive about the issue. "If appealing for fair play," he wrote nine years after the 1960 campaign, "in West Virginia [primary], accepting the invitations and questions of the Houston ministers, enlisting impartial Protestant clergymen to fight bigotry, and similar steps constitute 'exploiting' the issue, then exploit it we did. But not one of us in the Kennedy circle ever suggested that Nixon in the the election or Humphrey in the primaries was stirring up the issue. Not one of us ever asked people to vote for Kennedy to prove they were not bigots. . . ."[4]

The apparent manipulation of the religious issue by the Carter campaign seems, ironically, to have cut both ways, particularly among Catholics because of his stand on abortion and his advocacy of affirmative action, or reverse discrimination, for blacks. Both stands have angered northern white working-class Catholics. Carter pollster Patrick H. Caddell reported before the convention that the pro-abortion plank adopted by the Democratic Platform Committee angered many Catholics and his aides urged Carter to pick a Catholic as a way of offsetting Catholic defections.[5] Peter Bourne, another Carter aide, said he had spent, before the convention and after the adoption of the pro-abortion plank, an unusual amount of time responding to Catholic concerns. Tom Littlewood of the Chicago *Sun-Times* reported that Bourne mentioned "the candidate's Southern Baptist background, his opposition to parochial school aid and recent overtures to Jewish voters as contributing to Catholic uncertainty about Carter."[6]

Bourne did not mention the abortion issue or the attack on Carter by the National Conference of Catholic Bishops. The Catholic leadership was particularly critical of Carter since said that although he personally was opposed to abortion he would not support a constitutional amendment banning abortions. Carter's chief aide on issues, Stuart Eizenstat, who rode herd on the writing of the platform, tried to play down the attack on the platform, insisting that many Catholic Bishops did not support the National Conference view. The General Secretary of the National Conference angrily contradicted Eizenstat, saying he was "seriously misinformed."[7]

At a press conference announcing Senator Walter Mondale as his running mate, Carter said that "on abortion I would have personally favored different words on the platform. I didn't have any input or try to dominate the platform."[8]

The question that produced this Carterized response was triggered by a convention-floor attack on Carter by anti-abortion delegate Jim Killilea, who nominated the Right-to-Life candidate Ellen McCormack. Remarkably, the convention paid almost no attention to Killilea's slashing attack on Carter but instead, milled around and chatted throughout his appearance on the podium.

Killilea, a Catholic from Boston, suggested that it was strange for a "born-again" Christian to have such a callous disregard for the unborn. Referring to Carter as "Mr. X," the Right-to-Life delegate suggested that the Democratic Party was in "danger of becoming the party of abortion. Mr. X is the man who certainly will be the nominee of the Democratic Party," he added. "He is also the man who recently ordered the Democratic Platform Committee to adopt a strong pro-abortion plank. Ironically, back in Iowa, when Mr. X was but one of many candidates, he achieved his first success in the polls by persuading those who opposed abortion that he believed in their goals. It is now clear that those of us who supported Mr. X at that time were the victims of deception—deception from a candidate who looked us straight in the face and assured us he would never tell a lie."[9]

The contradictions expressed by Carter on the religious issue appear also within his own Southern Baptist circle. Traditionally, the strong commitment by Southern Baptists to separation of church and state has also meant that reforming one's self, and sinners, takes precedence over trying to reform society as a whole; politics did not enter into religious reform and salvation. But with the growth of Southern Baptist congregations outside the South and in large cities that has begun to change. "Increasingly 'new evangelicals' are writing articles in religious publications calling on fellow believers to throw their weight behind poor people and blacks. This approach also is being taken by a growing number of Baptist politicians, such as Carter. . . ."[10]

These shifts in emphasis raise the real issue of Jimmy Carter, even beyond his exploitation of the religious issue to gain the nomination. Does his quest for the presidency represent the first attempt to evolve a theology of power? If it does, and if this doctrine is based on the belief that the use of political power of the state can be justified on the grounds of Christian teaching, this step marks the emergence in America of what is known as Christian Socialism. Such a development would not be a complete surprise, since Carter's philosophical models have been prominent socialist theologians such as Niebuhr and Tillich, as explained in chapter three of this book.

Carter first enunciated this concept, foreign to American politics, when he asked his local minister, when he tried to discourage him from entering politics, "How would you like to be the pastor of a church with 80,000 members?"[11] Later, as a pair of friendly biographers observed, "Carter said as governor of Georgia, he regards his new social programs as 'an extension of the gospel—problem-solving combined with Christian charity."[12]

Jimmy Carter has evolved a theology of power with political leaders acting as priests at the head of the government. Both concepts—unlimited government power and the fusion of unlimited government with religious doctrine—were rejected by the founders of the American Republic and continue to be rejected by the voters of America.

The national trauma of the last ten years has produced among millions of Americans a hunger for decency and morality. Carter has successfully manipulated this hunger for his own ambitions. In the process, what he appears to be preaching is a doctrine not only dangerous but lethal to our liberty. It is a theological power doctrine in which the individual's salvation will be through the instrument of the all-powerful state headed by a charismatic Christian leader.

"Every time I hear a politician talk about morality," observed the theologian and writer Michael Novak, "my stomach tells me he is out to get me, even if at first I can't see how. . . . American coins have it correct: 'In God We

Trust.' Meaning, no one else. Not in political leaders. Not even in government. 'Our people are losing faith in America,' Nixon said. But America is not a religion."

Novak concludes, "We would do well to discipline our lust for morality. Better to strengthen our checks and balances, to lock our doors and to develop a reasonable tolerance for human fallibility, than to neglect political essentials in a temporary fit of purity."[13]

Since the time of the Founders of the American Republic, most of them southerners, political leaders (with few exceptions) have followed this formula. Now our traditional separation of the powers and functions of church and state are in jeopardy because of one politician's manipulations in his crusade for a new political priesthood.

NOTES

1. "U.S. Evangelism Revealing Its Long-Overlooked Power—Jimmy Carter Taps a Hidden Wellspring," *Chicago Sun-Times,* August 8, 1976.
2. "U.S. Evangelism."
3. "Giving Carter the Fish Eye," *Newsweek,* May 17, 1976.
4. Theodore C. Sorenson, *The Kennedy Legacy* (New York: Macmillan, 1969), p. 66.
5. "Carter Lacking Catholic Votes," *Raleigh* (N.C.) *News & Observer,* July 12, 1976.
6. "Carter Ponders Ways to Allay Catholic Doubts," *Chicago Sun-Times,* June 27, 1976.
7. "Carter Aide Scored on Abortion Remark," *The New York Times,* July 14, 1976.
8. Carter-Mondale press conference, Americana Hotel, New York City. ABC-TV, July 15, 1976, 10:45 am EDT.
9. ABC-TV Convention coverage, July 14, 1976, 9:40 pm EDT.
10. "The Southern Baptists—Who They Are, What They Believe," *U.S. News & World Report,* July 19, 1976.
11. *Why Not the Best?* p. 89.

12. Howard Norton and Bob Slosser, *The Miracle of Jimmy Carter*, p. 108.
13. "We Must Curb Our Lust for Morality in Politics: America's Illusion," *Washington Star*, April 11, 1976. Reprinted in *Congressional Record*, April 12, 1976, E1989.

"The North is saying to us, you got Carter, so come on in. . . . Come on in, you're really saying, and be like us."

—John Egerton
The Americanization of Dixie
1976

26

The New South vs. A Free South

"The New South" is a set of catch words that, like most catch words, implies and promises much, but explains little or nothing; this description is also the best summary of the political style and career of Jimmy Carter. A searching examination of the former Georgia governor's real views, aims, ambitions and programs forces this author to draw the conclusion that the "New South" is, in reality, a carbon copy of the "Old Liberal North." A triumph of "The New South," led by Carter, would be a tragic end to a *free South* and to the free United States.

Alliance with the values of the "Old Liberal North" was clearly implied by the location Carter chose for the launching of his fall presidential campaign on Labor Day 1976: Warm Springs, Georgia, the summer home of Franklin D. Roosevelt, who died there in April 1945. "Mr. Carter appears to have welded together [the] old Roosevelt coalition by his sheer lack of credibility," observed Jude Wanniski of the *Wall Street Journal*. "Conservatives in the party don't seem to believe him when he comes on like a liberal. And the party's liberals have been persuading themselves that he's just playing politics when he comes on like a conservative."[1]

Ultimately, one faction of the party must be fooled, and

the evidence suggests it will be the conservatives. This is particularly apparent in view of the remarkable range of alliances Carter has forged and the promises he has made to the northern liberals and labor union bosses. The South, which he has claimed because of his native-son status and his "born-again" Christian faith, appears to be confronted with a betrayal of its traditional values—just as Carter betrayed his native Georgia in 1970 after running as a conservative. Georgia newspaperman Millard Grimes contends that Carter could not have been reelected governor of Georgia after he switched from a conservative candidate to become a liberal governor in 1971. It was just as well Grimes believes, that he got into national politics: "Those who know him believe Carter's liberal sentiments reflect his own inner feelings. Nevertheless, it is clear that many Georgians felt slightly betrayed by Carter's seeming flip-flop."[2]

The Tennessee-born, Washington-based correspondent Frank van der Linden describes Carter as a "Yankee-style liberal disguised in a Confederate uniform." He offers as evidence Carter's favoring the repeal of right-to-work laws and other northern trade union goals. "The way would be cleared," he adds, "for massive union organizing campaigns in the twenty affected states, mostly in Dixie."[3]

If the unionized North is any forecast of what the South can expect, a Carter presidency would impose on the region the same sort of destructive national policies that have been bankrupting the North since the FDR New Deal. These policies have sent industry and population fleeing for relief to the South, for a saner and more civilized way of life. And so we face the inevitable question: Is Carter really a southerner?

The evidence we have shown here suggests that the only thing southern about Jimmy Carter is his birth and his soft drawl. Otherwise he is a naturalized liberal northerner with a belief in big-government social-engineering schemes. "Jimmy Carter," the southern historian Virginius Dabney commented after critiqueing this book in manuscript, "is not only in political philosophy contrary to the southern political leadership beginning with the Founders of the American Republic, but he is completely out of step with most of the contemporary political leadership in the South."

Historically, the Founders such as Thomas Jefferson, James Madison and others feared and distrusted the vigorous use of power—which Carter seeks. They were particularly hostile to a centralized national government—which Carter has made clear he will lead with vigor and purpose. Throughout the primary campaign, however, his purpose for wanting power and the end to which it would be used have been deliberately clouded in Carterized language that some have suggested is a unique and sophisticated form of political deception, if not outright lying. His wife tells us that Carter's political-power itch is particularly strong. "He can't wait to get his hands on it," Rosalynn Carter said of her husband's impatience even before the August Republican convention.[4]

"The itch," writes *Fortune*'s Juan Cameron, "has been bothering him at least since 1972, when he angled to become the running mate of the Democratic nominee, Senator George McGovern. After that attempt failed, he struck for the big prize on his own, armed with little beside a tough self-assurance, and a remarkable organizational talent. He was sustained by a fire in his belly that stems from his early life in the remoteness of rural Georgia, and by instincts born of a region where politics is both high theater and the most glamorous of vocations."[5]

The "fire in his belly" might be regional, but Carter's view of the world was shaped outside the southern experience when he deserted the land in favor of a career at sea that lasted eleven years. His engineering education at the U.S. Naval Academy at Annapolis apparently instilled in him two unsouthern characteristics: a narrow, almost blind, belief in structured and planned processes of thought and action, and an obedience to higher authority and power from a central directing source. Although southerners are historically the most law-abiding people in the nation, their political history shows a distrust and even resentment of centralized power and authority and of any attempts to impose a politically engineered structure on their individual lives. The southern educational experience, despite its growing dominance from Washington and northern liberal social engineers, takes two forms that few outside the South understand.

The first is the formal education that still clings to the classical ideal, however slender the thread, that broadens the individual and makes him a generalist rather than a specialist, such as an engineer. However anachronistic it may seem to some, southern formal education is still rooted in human moral values. "Such education," wrote the southern historian Richard Weaver, "was moral in the sense that it would give the youth a sound set of values. In accordance with the theory of the Greek thinker, it would teach one to approve and disapprove of the right objects in the right manner; or to display a set of correct sentiments determined by the code of the gentleman."[6]

This "code" put a premium on *morals,* meaning the respect a southerner paid to himself, and to *manners,* the respect paid to others. This influence can still be seen throughout the South today in an attitude many northerners sadly have lost: simple day-to-day civilized courtesies in their dealings with each other that range from a sincere "Thank you, come back and see us," to genuine respect and deference toward elders with "Yes, Ma'am," and "No, Sir." Southerners, black or white, have learned to live successfully with each other despite their hundred-year hardships—hardships that were experienced by no other region of the nation—because their culture and education have not yet abandoned obedience to this "code of the gentleman."

The second educational form in the South is formed by reason of geography, climate, economy and history. It is the least understood and least appreciated even by southerners—their informal self-education. The stereotyped "southern redneck" is much more sophisticated in the ways of the world and reality than his bookish and formally lettered northern brethren; his is an experience of living with the realities of the world, not with abstract theories. The fierce resistance of the "southern redneck" to the allegedly civilizing influences and sophisticated manipulative techniques of structured state education has been due almost exclusively to his instinctive distrust of anything that does not make sense. It is a shallow understanding by northern liberals, particularly my colleagues in the media, to write off the appeal of George Wallace or Lester Maddox merely to "racism." Rather, it is much more to the point and closer to the truth that such political personalities seem closer to what working-class voters perceive as having a "common-sense" approach to politics. Distrust of modern American education by those not formally educated is vindicated daily by the mounting evidence that a formal education today is a form of mental, moral and ethical suicide.

These two aspects of the southern educational experience, combined with religious tradition are the forces that have given the region its cohesion and stability. Stability has been fiercely maintained, despite the persistence of the race problem, which northerners have for a century and a half sought to solve for the South. "Many persons born outside of the culture," writes Weaver, "are never able to grasp [that] the southern resistance to 'education' and 'progress' is not just a negative thing—not merely a matter of torpor—but a positive one; it is part of the old pride in being a military, outdoor, unbookish 'sound' people, who prefer to be wrong in their own way rather than right in another's, and who have no desire to emulate the triumphs of New England. . . . It is instead the far more difficult task of winning them over to a completely different scale of values."[7]

When Jimmy Carter returned to Plains after an absence of nearly eleven years, the values he brought home with him were not those of a southerner but rather of a sophisticated specialist. He was an engineer with boundless personal ambition, an ex-Navy officer in search of a cause and profoundly influenced bv Adm. Hyman Rickover, an individual described by former Chief of Naval Operations Elmo Zumwalt as approaching a ruthless dictator.

These values and views are not those of a typical southerner, such as Carter's younger brother, Billy. "Everyone who gets to Plains," observe historian Bruce Nazlish and author Edwin Diamond, "knows Billy Carter. He is a warm, generous person—a good ole boy—with a four-wheel-drive van, and a beer can in hand before 11 am. He hasn't been inside a church in twenty years. A college dropout. He could not wait to break out of Plains to join the marines. At 4 am, the morning after his high-school graduation, he was on his way to boot camp. 'I wanted to be a badass' he told us.

"Billy Carter and James Earl Carter, Sr. knew how to relax, to take defeat. Jimmy Carter didn't know how. He was too proud, too self-righteous. And so he failed—himself and his father."[8]

Both Jimmy and Billy left Plains and returned. One never lost his touch with the land nor the southern values of their conservative father; the other did. "Jimmy's more liberal than I am," says Billy, "but I think it bothers him when I tell people that."[9] Billy is what northerners sneeringly call a typical "southern redneck" who has hard work written in his face, in his hard hands holding a beer can and in that short, muscular, powerful body that has not lost the marine "badass" swagger that hides a generous and giving nature.

In contrast, Jimmy is soft by comparison to the point of being almost effeminate. Although the campaign image has projected the hard-working peanut farmer who glories in the work ethic, Carter's appearance and mannerisms are those of a man who has not known hard manual labor for ten years or more. (This is not to deny that he worked to build the family business from 1953 until he ran for the state senate in 1963.) Billy perhaps explained this contradictory image when he revealed that for the last ten years he and his brother have not seen much of each other; Billy has been running the family peanut business while Jimmy was "off campaigning since 1966, really."[10]

Jimmy Carter's rejection of traditional conservative southern values is no less contradictory than was his rejection of his father. Carter has said he resigned the Navy in 1953 after he discovered the high regard with which his hard-working, conservative father was held in the community. It was probable that he had misjudged his own father, a common error in father-son relationships. It is not unlikely that his return to Plains was a mixture of genuine rediscovered admiration for his father and the means to an end to find his place in the world of Plains. But rather than fit in, there is every reason to believe that secretly he felt superior to his own family and neighbors by reason of his Annapolis education and world travels. "My daddy," he states, "worked hard and was a meticulous planner like me, but he was an exuberant man. He had an enjoyable life, like my brother Billy. If you know my brother Billy, then you've taken a major step toward knowing my father. . . ."[11]

Earl Carter, Sr. was, and his son Billy is, typically southern, reflecting a tolerance and acceptance of the world as it is. Their southern attitude of live-and-let-live is guided more by experience and common sense than by theory and abstractions. A difference between Jimmy and his father surfaces in his disagreement with his father over the race issue. "It was only after he left home," writes Carter biographer Leslie Wheeler, "that the mores of a segregationist society of his youth began to trouble him. He remembers only one racial argument with his father, which occurred when he was home on leave from submarine duty in 1950. After this, however, they both avoided the subject. Jimmy apparently thought too much of his father to challenge him on this issue."[12]

The conflict is important since it illuminates a larger landscape and provides a contrast of judgment based on experience and judgment based on theory.

Earl Carter, Sr. was the product of a southern society that suffered greatly as a result of northern moralizing over slavery. It is undeniable that slavery was a moral issue. It is equally undeniable—but not widely understood—that this country paid a catastrophic price because the abolitionists embraced a moralizing theory rather than a morality based on experience. The assumption before and after the War Between the States was that a solution to a deep-rooted problem could be engineered or legislated. The moral imperative of sweeping away slavery blinded the abolitionists to the complexity and consequences of their proposals, as well as to the understanding of what means could be employed to serve their purpose—to assimilate the blacks into Southern society or to implement their forced or voluntary resettlement back to their ancestral African homelands. The latter course was impractical, if not impossible; the former was a tragic failure, as post-Civil War reconstructionists found to their sorrow and disillusionment. Rather than blame their own theories of social engineering, the burden of blame was shifted to the shoulders of the blacks and to the allegedly evil and defeated southern political leadership.

Moral fanaticism, armed with nothing more than feelings and theories, provoked a shattering civil conflict, exhausted an entire civilization, and left blacks "free" without the means to self-sufficiency, the basis of true freedom. As a result, both North and South reached a compromise: segregation. The system was not, as intensely moralistic historians would have us believe, the product of some evil design to impose a new form of slavery on blacks. Rather, segregation, both that which is legally imposed and that which is accepted by custom and choice by both races, was the outgrowth of a nation exhausted by theories of equality that were unworkable under the circumstances. In short, segregation was an all but inevitable compromise after a bitter and brutal civil conflict, and the post-Civil War chaos provided bitter experience that the engineering of social, economic, and political relationships proved to be more complex, difficult and dangerous than its architects could have foreseen.

Without the paternalism of the master-slave condition, what political common ground could result? "The common ground that remained for political cooperation was *convenience* and *self-interest*," observed historians Weyl and Marina. "Hence, Tom Watson, the most eloquent Populist spokesman in favor of a Negro-White political alliance stressed *convenience* as its mainspring. Convenience, however, is temporary and changeable. When the apparent advantages of the Negro alliance were outweighed by its seeming liabilities, Tom Watson and many of his colleagues became transformed overnight into intolerant and brutal advocates of racial repression."[13]

Jimmy Carter's drive for national power is rooted in three theories that experience has shown to be failures: New Deal-type of federal programs, legislated racial justice for minorities, and social engineering by the national government.

This observation is supported by evidence of Carter's actions from the time he returned to Plains from the Navy in 1953 and began thinking of a political career. Carter first became actively involved in politics at the time of the Second Reconstruction effort, the civil rights movement of the early 1960s in the South. In his local community he both supported segregation and opposed it, the beginning of a pattern that persists to this day. As a Georgia state senator he was labeled as a liberal "New South" political personality in the style of John F. Kennedy, and when he ran for governor of Georgia in 1966 as an outright liberal, he lost. Switching his image, he conducted his 1970 Georgia gubernatorial campaign as a "redneck" and "outsider," only to switch again when elected and becoming a "New South" liberal. After supporting George McGovern in 1972 and seeking the number two spot, he switched again during his primary campaign to project the image of a southern conservative-to-moderate candidate running against Washington and the big bureaucracy. But it is clear that Jimmy Carter's presidency is already committed to greater national government programs and spending at the national level far beyond those first enacted by the FDR New Deal. He has also committed himself to follow the dictates of various liberal and radical groups who have their roots in the civil rights movement of the 1960s and the radical anti-war counterculture movement.

"Carter often says that Martin Luther King made his campaign possible," observes Garry Wills. "He means that King broke down the racist isolation of the South. But King as a symbol made Carter's rise easier for reasons that go beyond the civil rights movement. King was partly a cause and partly the result of the evangelicals' reentry into reform politics. Carter could not have risen so far so fast without the energies of this large social shift behind his effort."[13]

Carter's campaign theme as a "born-again" Christian, appealing to midwestern and southern whites, and his campaigning at the same time in black churches throughout the nation, is the most direct political expression of his appeal to the group called "evangelicals." The most vivid example of Carter's complete identity with the civil rights movement was seen when Rev. Martin Luther King, Sr., gave the benediction at the Democratic National Convention. "Surely," King proclaimed just prior to the entire convention holding hands and singing the civil rights hymn, "We Shall Overcome," "SURELY, the Lord sent Jimmy Carter to come out and bring America back where she belongs."[14]

Carter's campaign for the presidency is the outgrowth of a movement begun in the South in the 1960s that many charged at the time was after more than just civil rights. The aim was the implementation of more radical ideas that went beyond the issue of civil rights for blacks. In short, the Carter promises and programs in 1976, packaged in terms of Christian love, charity and compassion, are at once both radical and revolutionary. They also have a remarkable similarity to Christian Socialism (the forerunner of National Socialism in Europe beginning prior to World War I).

At the same time, Carter's projection as a "born-again" Christian of moderate-to-conservative views and as representative of the middle-class, church-going American culture is sharply contradicted by his highly visible associations with members of the counterculture, specifically, folk singer Bob Dylan, a hero of the anti-war New Left, and rock singer Gregg Allman, who has admitted daily use of hard drugs.[15]

Allman's manager is Carter's friend, the rock concert impresario Phil Walden. Allman, under Walden's orders, raised substantial amounts of money for Carter at a time during the primaries when his presidential bandwagon was in jeopardy because of a shortage of money. "Walden's chance to help came in the late fall of 1975," writes reporter Robert Sam Anson, "when a worried Jimmy Carter called him to say that unless the campaign could quickly raise $50,000, he would probably have to stop running. The result was a concert in Providence, Rhode Island, on November 25, 1975, featuring the Allman Brothers and Grinderswitch, both Walden groups. With Federal matching funds, the concert raised nearly $100,000 and put the Carter campaign back into operation. More Walden-arranged concerts, and one enormously successful telethon (it raised nearly $250,000), followed, bringing an estimated $400,000 ($800,000 after the federal matching funds were added) into the Carter coffers at the moment when it was most needed."[16]

The above figures are confirmed by the records of the Federal Election Commission. And Anson quotes a Carter aide as saying, "If it hadn't been for Phil, Jimmy would have been dead. We were just about through when Phil came along. Phil made everything possible. Iowa, New Hampshire. That was concert money, a lot of it. Jimmy owes Phil an enormous debt."[17]

All the evidence indicates that Jimmy Carter owes his crucial and successful campaign for the nomination to two groups that are anathema to the South: the radical elements of the labor union movement headed by United Auto Workers President Leonard Woodcock, and the counterculture, epitomized by the rock musicians organized by Phil Walden. We know what pledges and promises have been made to union bosses such as Woodcock: legislation that would open up the South to rapid unionization with repeal of the right-to-work laws. We do not know what pledges and promises, if any, Carter has made to the New Left counterculture groups.

The evidence and the record suggest an explosive combination of elements when pieced together:

• A presidential candidate consumed with boundless ambition for power and apparently willing to switch positions and sides to achieve that end, while professing never to tell a lie or mislead the public.

• A political personality who has almost no solid experience, and who misrepresents his one term as governor as an achievement when the public record says otherwise.

• A candidate whose political ideas and programs are rooted in the failures of the past; yet he has forged alliances with radical and revolutionary groups who could carry an explosive, social-political experiment beyond the point that would seem prudent. Such an experiment could end in greater strife and conflict than was ever produced in the past.

• A candidate who has had a campaign of marrying a program of New Racism, defined as special favors for minority groups backed by the power of national government, with a religious evangelicalism that is a formula for the suicide of freedom and social harmony between the races and religions.

• A political personality who professed to want to strengthen and defend the American family, only to advocate government policies that have undermined the family unit. Specifically, this points to his political alliances with and his pledges of billions to the educational establishment, which seeks to replace parental responsibility with control by educators intent on instilling ethics and beliefs contrary to traditional American doctrines.

The highly explosive nature of this combination is made more so by Carter's personality and a belief in power as a tool for social-political engineering.

Carter himself is the political product of a one-party system in the South. His election as president would mean the consolidation of complete control of the national government by one party—a view held by a northern journalist and a southern journalist. ". . . all I can be certain of," observed Richard Reeves of *New York* magazine, "is that Carter is the product of a far different political system than the one people like me know. It certainly seems possible, however, that a southern presidency and the terminal spasms of the Republican party may bring the nation into a period of one-party government something like what was practiced for generations in Georgia and other southern states.

"We can see," he adds, "a Carter presidency with an overwhelmingly Democratic Congress in which the relevant questions will not be about party but about whether a legislator is 'Carter' or 'anti-Carter.' "[18]

John Crown, columnist for *The Atlanta Journal,* observed that he would have "serious doubts that [Carter] would have the guts to stand up to a Democratic Congress. It would make splinters of the Democratic platform plank that promised a good relationship between executive and legislative branches.

"Moreover, I believe that the knowledge that President Ford would veto foolish legislation places a restraint of sorts on that sort of legislation going through Congress.

"With Mr. Carter in the Oval Office, a man who finds himself in agreement with starry-eyed Mr. Mondale, there would be no restraint."[19]

Despite the much promoted "New South" and the candidacy of Jimmy Carter as a representative of that development as a final reconciliation for a nation divided by the Civil War, the evidence suggests differently. The "New South" is to be nothing more than a carbon copy of the "Old Liberal North." In the so-called New South the northern liberals have found a political formula to shatter the transformation of the South from a one-party to a two-party political region. Jimmy Carter is the means and the end of northern liberal Democrats to bring about the establishment of one-party government, nationally.

This movement is particularly crucial for northern liberals who have watched as the South and the Sunbelt

States grow in economic and political power with industry and population fleeing the North for the more conservative and free regions of the nation not overwhelmed by social and racial conflict and economic stagnation brought about by decades of liberal social engineering.

The candidacy of Jimmy Carter, like his campaign and rise to national prominence, is not what its promoters and supporters claim. Rather, it is a historic, political movement of a radical minority bent on seizing and holding absolute power.

The issue, therefore, in 1976 is not a "New South" but a *free South* and a free nation. The southern author of *The Americanization of Dixie,* John Egerton, senses in Carter's rise to national prominence a danger to the cultural traditions of the South, but he ignores the political implications. "Everything that was happening was to wrong," he states of the race issue, "but it just centered on one thing. And I thought that if we could turn that one thing around, we would have it all. Now, I don't know. Don't get me wrong. I feel really good about Carter, but what worries me is everything that is going to happen to the South because of him. The South is going to become a fad. . . . We're giving up the virtues and keeping the vices. The thing that I've always feared is about to happen: the reunion is going to take place, but it'll happen on someone else's terms. Your terms. . . . The North is saying to us, you got Carter, so come on in. Just one thing, though. You got to borrow your money from northern banks, get your know-how from the North, get your way of thinking from the North. Come on in, you're really saying, and be like us."[19]

Jimmy Carter's betrayal of the South is a betrayal of the nation founded two centuries ago in 1776 on the new and revolutionary notion that men had been governed too much. Throughout these two centuries the South has sought to uphold the original founding principles that a nation's citizens were individuals who should be given the widest latitude to develop individually, and that tolerance of diversity among people was the basis for human progress and happiness. The South, more than any other part of the nation, has clung to the old virtues while the North has rushed headlong into the mass faceless society based on the idea that equality could maintain freedom, order and progress.

The northern urban areas today are not only a repudiation of that belief, but their sickness and stagnation is the expression and evidence of a deadly disease which the South has these many decades found ways to inoculate itself against. The social, cultural and political serum has been a set of values and beliefs that transcend race—that appeal to the spirit of all men and women who truly value the idea of tolerance and diversity among individuals and who disdain conformity to mass ideas enforced by massive power.

The South has the longest tradition in America of tolerating eccentrics. It is a region hardened by a hundred-year history that vainly and heriocally sought to come to grips and solve, in its own way, one of the most difficult and dangerous of human problems: race relations. On the record, the evidence suggests that it did not retreat in the face of that staggering human problem. Rather, it made a supreme effort, as befits its long cultural tradition of humaneness and consideration for feelings and sensibilities, that other cultures and other civilizations have not had the courage to confront. The fact the South never turned on blacks in a never-ending program of genocide but sought to work out, based on experience and not theory, some compromise that would promote an imperfect solution speaks most eloquently in its behalf. But in confronting its problems, it has had precious little help and sympathy from northerners who did not pass through the ordeal and burden of the South's experience.

Now, two centuries after the founding of the Republic by southern political leaders, and on the eve of the centennial year 1877, when the last federal forces were withdrawn from the South in the wake of attempts at reconstruction, the southerner Jimmy Carter is leading a coalition of power brokers in a New Reconstruction effort founded on a theory of social democracy not in the history, culture and tradition of the South.

Carter promises the South and the nation, bread and bureaucracy, even while most Americans, northerners and southerners alike, hunger for the confirming grace of how to live fully, spiritually and with purpose as individuals. "The Old South," writes historian Richard Weaver, "may indeed be a hall hung with splendid tapestries in which no one would care to live; but from them we can learn something of how to live."[20]

NOTES

1. "A Peanut in a Poke," *Wall Street Journal,* July 16, 1976.
2. "From a Georgian Newsman: A Cautious Dissent," *Los Angeles Times,* August 29, 1976.
3. "Jimmy Carter: Yankee Style Liberal in Confederate Uniform?" United Features Syndicate, August 9, 1976.
4. Juan Cameron, ". . . And Now to Carterize the White House," *Fortune,* August, 1976.
5. ". . . And Now to Carterize the White House."
6. Weaver, *The Southern Tradition at Bay* (New Rochelle, N.Y.: Arlington House, 1968), p. 78.
7. *The Southern Tradition at Bay.*
8. "Thrice Born—A Psychohistory of Jimmy Carter's 'Rebirth,'" *New York,* August 30, 1976.
9. "Billy Runs the Carter Empire," *People,* July 19, 1976.
10. "As a Leader, Georgian Is Strong and Capable; Flaw: Huge Ambition," *Wall Street Journal,* July 12, 1976.
11. "Thrice Born," *New York.*
12. Leslie Wheeler, *Jimmy Who?*
13. Garry Wills, "The Carter Question," *New York Review of Books*, August 5, 1976.
14. "Black Oratory: Roots in Religion, Future in Politics," *Washington Post,* July 23, 1976.
15. "Allman Testifies in Drug Probe," *Rolling Stone.*
16. "The Capricorn Connection," *New Times,* September 3, 1976.
17. "The Capricorn Connection."

18. Richard Reeves, "With Georgia a One-Party State, Can the Nation Be Far Behind?" *New York*, August 9, 1976.
19. Robert Sam Anson, "Looking for Jimmy: A Journey Through the South, Rising," *New Times*, (date).
20. Weaver, *The Southern Tradition at Bay*, p. 396.

Appendix 1

VIEWPOINT # 3229, PRESENTED BY JEFFREY ST. JOHN FRIDAY, NOVEMBER 28, 1975

The Democratic Party made a crusade out of deploring and damning campaign dirty tricks and unethical conduct of political candidates. But recently Florida Democrats held a convention in Orlando.

During the convention former Georgia Governor Jimmy Carter emerged the winner of a straw poll among the delegates. Governor George Wallace finished a poor third. The press reported this as Carter's Presidential band wagon flattening Wallace in Florida. Carter's star is rising and Wallace's is fading, we have been told.

We did some investigating and found the straw poll was rigged in Carter's favor. First, a "by invitation only" mailing was sent out to Florida Democrats. Only token Wallace supporters were on the list. Second, we found that the registration fee and costs to attend the convention were so high a Wallace working class supporter could not afford to attend. Third, we have learned the Democratic National Committee has, for two years, paid the expenses of four principal aides of Governor Carter. Clearly evidence that the Democrats have been grooming Governor Carter for two years as the man to stop Wallace.

The rigging of the straw poll at a recent Florida Democratic convention in Carter's favor comes under the heading of political dirty tricks decried by the Democrats during Watergate.

Are the Democrats so fearful of Wallace that they must stoop to rigging polls and feeding such phony results to a gullible media?

With Viewpoint, I'm Jeffrey St. John.

Appendix 2

Jeffrey St. John:

The Watergating Of George Wallace

WASHINGTON—"This vote in Florida," contends former Georgia Gov. Jimmy Carter of a Nov. 16 presidential straw ballot at a Democratic state convention, "was the first major test of strength in the South. It's a good indication of what's going to happen in 1976."

This statement has a double-edged meaning. Carter meant it to convey that his clobbering of George Wallace in the presidential straw ballot was a forecast of his rising political fortunes. Of 1,035 delegates who voted, Carter took 697 votes, Pennsylvania Gov. Milton Shapp came in second with 60, and Wallace received 57.

For two days following the Orlando meeting, the national television networks, the wire services and influential newspapers like the Washington Star forecast that Carter's straw-vote victory posed a serious challenge to Wallace. However, a week-long investigation by this columnist has led to the conclusion that the convention was rigged in Carter's favor. Indeed, it raises the question whether Wallace will get similar treatment from other Democratic Party officials, for, in Carter's words, "It's a good indication of what's going to happen in 1976." Here is what we have uncovered:

1. Since 1973 the Democratic National Committee, still heavily influenced and controlled by the extreme left-wing policies of 1972 presidential candidate George McGovern, chose Carter as the candidate to blunt Wallace's bid for the presidential nomination.

This even went so far as the DNC paying the expenses of three aides of Carter: Hamilton Jordon, Rick Hutcheson and Knox Pitts. All three served as advance men for Carter who stumped the state no less than 22 times since January, 1975—beginning 11 months before the November convention. During Carter's visits he met with the county chairmen who, on orders from Democratic State Chairman Ann Cramer, handpicked pro-Carter delegates. A copy of a letter signed by Mrs. Cramer shows she specifically directed the county chairmen to select the delegates. To insure further political solidarity for Carter, the party's first state convention in 75 years was "by invitation only" and such invitations went not to rank-and-file Democrats but to party leaders. As a result only a handful of pro-Wallace leaders made it to the convention.

The cost of the three-day affair was well out of the range of working-class Wallace supporters in any event, running as high as $250 for a couple.

2. The actual delegate count at the convention was 1,700—although 665 didn't vote. State Chairman Cramer included "other designated groups" like blacks, women and the state's Young Democrats, the latter who gave Carter a solid bloc of 60 votes in the straw balloting! The official invitation reads, "It's great that you have been selected," but is very unclear how the delegation process took place. It is clear, however, that the majority of the delegates came from major urban areas of Florida which have always been anti-Wallace. In contrast, Wallace lost a similar straw ballot in 1972 but went on to carry every county in Florida in the 1972 primary.

3. Democratic National Committeeman Norman Bie, a Clearwater, Fla., lawyer and a pro-Wallace delegate to the convention, labeled the straw vote "a clear setup," although he went out of his way to absolve Mrs. Cramer of being anti-Wallace and a party to the straw-vote rigging.

"It was just good old-fashioned politics," he said in an interview. "I don't see anything new about rigging a poll to show you are ahead. John F. Kennedy did it and Lyndon Johnson did it and so does every aspiring politician but Wallace. This is why I support him after years as a Roosevelt, Truman and Stevenson Democrat."

Bie believes that the Nov. 16 setup indicates what the Wallace people can expect from the party leaders of the DNC in the primaries next year. All this from the same political party that made a moral crusade out of political dirty tricks by Nixon Republicans during Watergate.

Copley News Service, Nov. 28, 1975

Appendix 3

December 8, 1975

Mr. Jody Powell
Press Secretary
Carter for President Committee
Post Office Box 1976
Atlanta, Georgia 33301

Dear Mr. Powell:

Pursuant to our telephone conversation this afternoon, I am enclosing a copy of my Copley News Service column that is distributed to some 1,600 papers in the U. S. and overseas containing the names of principal aides of Governor Carter who I asserted have had their expenses paid by the Democratic National Committee while working on behalf of Governor Carter's candidacy. (On my television commentary, I'd said there were four individuals—inadvertently omitted from the column, the fourth is Marc Cutright.)

I would, as I stated to you on the phone, be willing to issue a retraction in my column and in the regular Viewpoint commentary on WRAL-TV, Raleigh, North Carolina, if I am provided a notarized statement from each of those named that they have not had their expenses or salaries paid by the Democratic National Committee in the last 24 months, and a notarized statement from Gov. Carter's finance chairman that no one else in the Governor's campaign committee has received payment of any kind from the DNC.

Cordially,
/s/ Jeffrey St. John

enc.

P.S. I do understand that you have the opportunity to reply to WRAL-TV Viewpoint and have so been offered such time by Mr. James Goodmon, president of WRAL-TV Raleigh.

Appendix 4

'Don't Tread on Me'

By Jeffrey St. John

"Men born to freedom," observed Justice Brandeis, "are naturally alert to repel invasion of liberty by evil-minded rulers. The greatest danger to liberty lurks in insidious encroachment by the men of zeal, well-meaning but without understanding."

The zealous promoters of the political glamor stock called the new populism do not understand the inherent nature of government as a naked monopoly on physical force which increasingly has violated individual liberty. Such monopolistic power has plundered the private citizen's purse for the benefit of any group that can control and manipulate the machinery of government. Such legalized larceny has been justified in the name of social-economic equality.

Now the new populists posture as enemies of corporate power and of "excessive government power." Yet they make it perfectly clear that they are prepared to use the power of government for a social and economic program to benefit a political coalition that will help them wrest power from what they believe is the "establishment" or "big boys who get all the breaks."

The special privilege and subsidy enjoyed by a host of groups is the direct result of government power. Nevertheless, the new populism proposes to use government to enforce a program of "soak the rich." Why use the power of government to soak any group or grant any segment of society, rich, poor, corrupt, individual or groups, special subsidy or privilege?

What the new populism portends is an update of Marxian class warfare, the prize being the political power to penalize and punish one group for the benefit of another. Big business, if not all business, is the clear target of the new populist. No rational distinction is made between a company or organization that has grown to giant status by competition as opposed to one that has benefited from government subsidy and special franchise. Instead of consistently arguing for a free market economy—destroyed by government intervention that has brought about an inequality that the new populism rightfully deplores

—the central thrust is to fashion bolder and more blunt government policies that could carry the current "mixed" economy of controls and freedom to total government command of the economy—all in the name of reform.

What is dangerous and demagogic about the new populism is its reliance, as George Wallace is doing, on seeking scapegoats for problems that were created by government in the first place. Such scapegoat politics were precisely the same premises that discredited the old populism, which degenerated into virulent racial and religious hatred. The old populism was founded on the false belief that the economic woes of the post-Civil War period were products of Jewish bankers, newly enfranchised blacks, and the rise of Catholicism to challenge the basic Protestantism of the nation. In short, the old populism was united by an explosive combination of economic envy, race and religious bigotry.

The new populism was influenced by Marxist economic thinking, and incorporated piecemeal first, the old populists, then the Progressives, the New Deal, and now the New Left who are, in reality, the new populists seeking to broaden their political appeal by embracing working-class Americans. It remains to be seen whether the new populism, like the old, breaks out with the old typhoid of intolerance and hatred.

What the nation needs is not a new populism founded on fear, frustration and envy, but a new radicalism founded on the original philosophy of the Founders of the American Republic: individual liberty, limited government and free, uncontrolled economic enterprise. This means a constitutional separation of politics from economics, much as we now have a separation of church and state. The new radicalism does n[illegible] look to Europe for its philosophical inspiration, but to the American Revolution of 1776 and the idea that individuals are sovereign with rights and that law, rather than license for legalized larceny, is the only legitimate function as a protector of life, liberty and property.

The new populism's battle cry is "Power to the People." The new radicalism rooted in 1776 replies: "Don't Tread On Me."
The New York Times, May 2, 1972, Op. Ed. page

Appendix 5

Executive Department
Atlanta 30334

Jimmy Carter
GOVERNOR

January 29, 1971

Mr. Reed Larson
Executive Vice President
National Right to Work Committee
1900 L Street, N. W.
Washington, D. C. 20036

Dear Mr. Larson:

Thank you very much for your letter of January 13 relative to the Right to Work Law.

I stated during my campaign that I was not in favor of doing away with the Right to Work Law, and that is a position I still maintain.

Again, let me express to you my appreciation for your letter and the information contained therein.

Sincerely,

Jimmy Carter

Jimmy Carter

JC/mjp

About the Author

Jeffrey St. John was educated and began his journalism career in the South. As a veteran political journalist, columnist and broadcast news commentator, he has covered national politics from Washington since the Eisenhower years, specializing on the White House and Congress.

On the national scene he writes a syndicated column for the Copley News Service and is the National Correspondent for the Panax Newspapers. In addition he contributes to the editorial pages of the nation's leading newspapers, among them *The New York Times, Newsday, Philadelphia Inquirer,* and *The Los Angeles Times.*

At the regional level he is a syndicated broadcast news commentator for WRAL-TV and The North Carolina News Network, Raleigh, North Carolina. He also is seen regularly on WRC-TV, Washington, D.C. in the regular commentary series "About Washington."

He is the recipient of a coveted Emmy, awarded by the National Academy of Arts & Sciences for his public affairs TV program "Opinion Plus" and for his Copley column he was awarded the George Washington Medal, Freedoms Foundation, Valley Forge, Penn.

For over three years he was a CBS Radio-TV "Spectrum" commentator and was, for a year, a regular on the NBC-TV "Today" Show.

His previously published work, *Countdown to Chaos: Chicago, August 1968,* was an analysis of the riots at the 1968 Democratic Convention, which he had forecast two weeks prior to the disorders in the publication *Barron's.* He is also the author of the monograph, "History As a Political Weapon," published in June of 1976 by The Heritage Foundation of Washington, D.C.

He characterizes himself as "an independent conservative" in the tradition of the Founding Fathers of the American Republic and John Randolph of Roanoke, the original architect of the South's historic resistance to federal control of the States of the Union.

He lives and works with his wife, Kathryn, in historic Charlotte County, Virginia, near the North Carolina border.